KICKING

KICKING

Following the Fans to the Orient

David Willem

MAINSTREAM
PUBLISHING

EDINBURGH AND LONDON

First published in Great Britain in 2002 by
MAINSTREAM PUBLISHING (EDINBURGH) LTD
7 Albany Street
Edinburgh EH1 3UG

ISBN 1 84018 623 2

A catalogue record for this book is available from the British Library

Typeset in Caslon and FF Din

Printed in Great Britain by
Mackays of Chatham Ltd

FOR Z, R & F

CONTENTS

TOKYO – SAITAMA
England 1 Sweden 1   9

SAPPORO
Argentina 0 England 1   33

OSAKA
Japan 1 Russia 0
Nigeria 0 England 0   67

NIIGATA PART ONE
Ireland 1 Cameroon 1   95

NIIGATA PART TWO
England 3 Denmark 0   115

TOKYO
Japan 0 Turkey 1   143

TOKYO – SHIZUOKA
England 1 Brazil 2   163

TOKYO – SAITAMA

England 1 Sweden 1
2–5 June

THIS IS HOW JAPAN GETS YOU. I AM STANDING ON A BALCONY overlooking a domestic garden. There are familiar vegetables and strange, unidentifiable vegetables growing in the dusty soil. It is early, the sun not yet too hot, and a woman is hanging out clothes on a line to dry. And I think, 'How close to nature these people are. Look how she uses the sun and wind to dry her family's clothes.'

It is a few seconds before I realise that hanging out your laundry in the open air is not a peculiarly Japanese habit. But this is what happens when you spend any time in Japan. You start thinking very odd thoughts indeed.

It was the same for the England supporters who came here for the World Cup: what had been natural to them began to look very odd, and what had been odd began to look very natural. Instead of being treated like pariahs, as had happened at previous tournaments, they began to think that they were actually welcome in Japan. And so they too began to think very strange thoughts. 'Shouldn't all World Cups be like this?' they asked each other. 'I mean, if you are going to host the World Cup and invite the teams to visit your country, shouldn't you also make the fans welcome, just like Japan has done, even if they are English?'

What was doubly strange about the effect that Japan had on the English was that nobody had anticipated it. Before the tournament had started everyone was complaining that it would be too expensive, that the Japanese police and the people would be terrified of us because of the hooligans, that the only connection they had with the world of football was the way in which, like the sports pages, their books are read backwards. And even after the tournament had started, we were still complaining: about there being nowhere to watch the games on television, that the Japanese were contributing nothing to the atmosphere, that Japan had not so much embraced the World Cup as diverted itself around it. 'You wouldn't know there was a World Cup going on in this country,' was the complaint on everyone's lips.

What no one had anticipated was the slow burn of Japanese hospitality. It doesn't feel that warm, and you don't realise it's affecting you until one morning you wake up slightly touched by the heat. And despite the Factor 48 layer of cynicism in which we English habitually cover ourselves, it got us all in the end.

....

Somehow I have contrived to arrive in Tokyo at 5 a.m. on the day that England play Sweden. The sky above the station entrance turns from grey to blue in about 30 seconds. The kids returning from a night out call goodbye, and for a moment the cawing crows above them are louder than the city. There is litter on the streets, and adverts on every vertical surface that is not a window, and sometimes on the windows too. Even the ground is etched with ribbed and yellow tiles for the blind to follow. This is how it is for the next four days. The mind never stops in Tokyo. Information is everywhere. It comes through every channel. Your eyes check backwards and forwards over flickering neon, squiggles of meaning you cannot read, and fragments of English you cannot understand. The only long-distance sight line is into the focus-less sky. Your hearing is pressured by recorded announcements, loudhailer instructions and shouting hawkers. Your sense of smell perverted by alien excretions, your taste by food you cannot name. You are constantly balancing in lifts and on escalators and on the very earth itself as you swerve round the endless surge of people. Only your sense of touch remains aloof. Your hand goes ungrasped by men and your cheeks unkissed by women. They stay at nodding distance, bowing, and it leaves you more alone.

If London is the great wen, then Tokyo is the great where, for you never have any idea where you are. There is nothing to orientate yourself by, no river to tell you north or south. The sun goes so high so quickly that it is difficult to get your bearings. There is just a bay that you never see. Nowhere looks more than 50 years old. And even if you know the history it only stays in your head: the bombing of the city by the Americans, the great earthquake of 1923, that it only became the capital in the nineteenth century. All you see is ever-moving modernity, a broad blade of 50 years chopping and churning everything in its wake.

Ah, Tokyo, the infernal city. In every building there are seven floors, and on every floor there are seven bars, and in every bar there are seven hostesses, and for every hostess there are seven clients. The mind cannot fathom the multiples of people, the number of ways that each one could lead you through the city. Everything is up and down: bars in the sky and shopping arcades scraped into the ground. I had never realised until I came to Tokyo that being English meant liking flatness, and completeness, or at least the possibility of completeness. But it took only a few minutes with a map of Tokyo to realise that there is no way, however long I stay, that I will ever know more than a fraction of a fraction of what is in this city.

It is a city without a city centre. Instead it has tens of separate districts, each with a separate identity and reached by separate railways: national, private and subway lines for which no ticket covers all. And I am in Ikebukuro: the district for shopping in tall buildings.

It is 5.30 a.m. and in the space of 20 minutes I see, among hundreds going down into the station: a tall transvestite in jeans cut like cowboy chaps to reveal G-string panties and suspenders; a muscled goat-bearded man in clothes more utilitarian than Muji's carrying in one hand a wooden samurai sword and in the other the wrist of a struggling woman; a 20-strong gang of buskers of whom only four or five have guitars; paralytic youths being dragged home by their friends; and white faces who ignore mine. This is what you must do in Tokyo: pretend you have not seen the foreigners.

We must be a sight to the Japanese, us foreigners, with our hair, eyes and skin in such a range of shades, sticking out like sore thumbs and yet ignoring each other's presence. We must look as ridiculous as a reptilian race of aliens wandering through London and failing to acknowledge another of our kind. We don't, because to show that you have noticed another foreigner, or worse, to speak to them, is to show yourself up as a know-nothing just off the plane.

KICKING

11

But there are foreigners in Ikebukuro I cannot ignore. There is an Englishman, Rob. He is from Watford, a Japan-head, shorthaired, with an earring, a friend of my brother. I will go to the match with him and his mate. But first I must go to sleep on their hotel room floor.

We go nowhere until late in the afternoon and then begin the hour's journey by subway out of Tokyo to the stadium in the suburbs. From the raised tracks you can see the city change character. At first the gaps between the buildings are credit-card sized, but the buildings shrink and the gaps widen the further out we go, until there are tiny gardens and the odd copse of green among all the beige, brown, russet and grey of the houses. Rice paddies appear among the sprawl much sooner than expected; the shoots of the rice are like green iron filings magnetised into regularity, the paddies uniformly rectangular but more natural looking than the fractal landscapes of the golf courses.

Japan does not have a green-belt policy, it is more a green-belt and urban braces policy. There is never a point when the town becomes the country or the country the town.

There are other English on the train, but it is impressive how quickly we have adapted to the Tokyo take-no-notice-of-other-foreigners rule. Even in our white or red tops, we continue to ignore each other. It is only as we get close to the station near the stadium that we begin to acknowledge each other's presence, and then suddenly there are too many of us to bother.

It is the noise that gets you first when you come out of the station, but it's not the noise of the English. The stadium is another 15 minutes' bus ride away. It's the Japanese, making official noise. Unofficial noise is near silence in Japan. There was a young woman standing on our platform as we changed trains. She was trying to attract the attention of an older man on the other platform, but at the same time was trying to remain inconspicuous: a feat that no one can manage.

'*Yoshida-san,*' she whispered in a voice that he would not notice if he was standing next to her. '*Yoshida-san.*'

She kept this up for a couple of minutes until I was tempted to cup my hands and bellow his name for her. Finally, and not through any result of her exertions, his gaze finally rested on her and they were able to wave and bow.

Official noise is very loud. It is no more than 15 yards between the station exit and the free bus to the stadium, but there are police with loudhailers and several red-shirted stewards to yell you the way. Adding to this cacophony are the newspaper hawkers in black and white shirts, and the camera and snack vendors shouting their wares.

But the English are still quiet. I had wondered before I came how we would dress, whether there would be any mythic equivalent of the leprechaun costumes I had seen the Irish wear, and if so what would it be. I had heard of bowler hats being given away by national newspapers for England fans to wear, which, by recalling both the dystopian violence of *A Clockwork Orange* and the stiff formality of the 1950s, made dual and contradictory reference to what it means to be English. But I see no characters from England's mythic or bureaucratic past that day. On the free bus to the stadium there are two people dressed as David Seaman with ponytail wigs and drooping moustaches who seem by their accent to be American, and there is one hot, unhappy lad wearing a Mad Hatter's top hat of red and white fake fur. But they are exceptional. The English in general favour oriental additions to their uniform of red or white. Instead of retreating towards some essential self, they meet the Japanese head on. Some wear coolie hats or rubber hairpieces in the style of samurai topknots, or oriental bandannas with Japanese characters and the cross of Saint George.

The stadium stands proud and modern on the flattened horizon like an airport terminal. The bus speeds towards it along empty roads through the rural-suburban mix of rice paddies, houses, roadside restaurants, vending machines and convenience stores. It only slows as we reach the vast complex, the acres of tarmac bus-park where yellow-uniformed stewards guide the driver in.

It is the number of people that gets you, but like the noise it isn't the English, it is the Japanese. Hundreds of stewards direct the crowds while hundreds of police patrol among them. The Japanese have thrown thousands of people at this event and the extent of their human resources is extraordinary. So, too, is the rigorousness of the layered levels of security. Helicopters patrol the sky. Female stewards check my ticket before I get onto the bus, and then again as I enter the outer ring around the stadium, then my bags and possessions as I enter the inner ring, and finally my ticket once more before I step up onto the terraces. It is unlike any event I have ever been to.

KICKING

But it is like another place we have all just passed through. With its buses, ticket checks, baggage checks and stewardesses showing you to your seat, the stadium is a model of an airport, and your ticket is at once ticket and visa and passport to the World-Cup-world.

It is a strange place, this World-Cup-world. It overlaps but is not the same as the real world. Nations like Sweden that hardly register in the everyday consciousness of the English assume a profile out of any proportion to their place in the real world, while the disparity between the American giant outside and the dwarf that exists in World-Cup-world is one of the most attractive things you will ever see. But the best thing about World-Cup-world, and really why we have all come, is that you can be as nationalistic as you want to be without condemnation. It is about the only place where hurling abuse at foreigners, wrapping yourself in the flag, and the repetitious saluting of England with two-handed fascist salutes is not just acceptable, but is regarded as normal. Behaviour which back in the real world would be seen as indicative of mental disturbance or extreme right-wing politics here becomes kind of fun. It is like pantomime for grown-ups. Even the shouts of 'man-on' sound like 'behind you'. We boo the Swedish team as they are announced and cheer the English. And now the English are making some noise.

We sing the national anthem lustily, and there is a small, unauthorised addition inserted into the text by a small minority of the crowd. Instead of singing 'God save our gracious Queen, Long live our noble Queen, God save the Queen, Da da da daa, Send her victorious . . .', the official version, some of the crowd replace the rising 'das' with the words 'No surrender'.

This is a reference to another England song, which again is only performed by a small proportion of the crowd. It goes nicely to the tune of 'Sing Hosanna!':

> There's a George in my heart, keep me English.
> There's a George in my heart, I say.
> There's a George in my heart, keep me English.
> Keep me English 'til my dying day.
> No surrender! No surrender! No surrender to the IRA (scum)!
> No surrender! No surrender! No surrender to the IRA (scum)!

KICKING

14

Whether you like its sentiments or not, as a song it really works. The happy-clappy religious tune contrasts neatly with the uncompromising message; the words of the verse, all that 'I say, George', speak of a gentlemanly past while the 'scum' in the chorus doesn't, and the inclusion of 'No surrender' in the national anthem actually fits quite well with the sentiments of 'Send her victorious, happy and glorious'.

But this is just too far to the right for the majority of the crowd, although many more of them are happy to taunt the Scots with 'Bonnie Scotland, bonnie Scotland, what's the weather like at home?' From the laughter that greets this chant you can tell that there are quite a few here who have never heard this before, and their laughter is indulgent and perhaps nervous, because they can see that the individuals who were most prominent in singing it are the uncompromisers who have just sung 'No Surrender'. Nobody mentions Wales, however, because Wales doesn't exist in World-Cup-world.

So instead of attacking the Swedes (who even in World-Cup-world aren't *that* important) the first thing we do is turn our attention to the matter of the Union.

Virtually everyone do-do, do-do-do-do-dos along to theme to *The Great Escape*, the tune provided by the brass band somewhere above us at the back of the stands. You can tell the people who are at their first England match. They are covertly watching everyone else to see how to behave and slowly getting used to the clapping and double-armed salute which accompanies the chant of 'In-ger-land'.

Somewhere you can find your own level of nationalism in all of this: from condemning Irish republicanism, to taunting Scotland, to supporting England, through double-armed fascist-style salutes (although there is not much else you can do with your hands in an enclosed space that doesn't look like a fascist salute) to merely clapping. From xenophobia to nationalism to patriotism to just supporting the team, you can take your pick, and the crowd distributes itself along this continuum with the majority falling somewhere between nationalism and patriotism.

This is how the crowd behaves on a large scale, visible as a mass on the monitors and as background noise on the microphones, but around me in the seats behind the goal the crowd fragments into

KICKING

15

individuals. A voice directly behind me maintains an amused but not amusing commentary throughout the match. For him, individual players, particularly Heskey, are singled out and treated as characters whose fumbling attempts to play at this level are filled with pathos. 'Go on, that's it, try a pass, don't worry, there'll be another chance. You're doing OK, at least your mum's proud.' And when the ball boys are slow in getting a ball back onto the pitch, 'What are you doing? Making your dad proud that he can see you on the telly?'

To my right literally and politically is one of the 'No Surrender' singers. He had come to stand on the gangway. He is big faced and 40-ish, huge with a tall, proud stance. He has a permanent expression of sneering amusement, as if to be him was the best possible state any human being could aspire to, as if he is amazed at the inadequacies of people who are not like him and the inadequacy of anybody's right to check his behaviour. Alongside him stands a smaller man of the same age, no less proud of his physical presence, which is fit and muscular. He has short, balding hair but it does not make him look old. Together they banter with loud 'fucks' and 'cunts', joined by a third man two rows behind who shouts at one point 'He's rolling a joint!' The smell of marijuana drifts across from the first man, but no scent of peace and love. So they shout to each other across the crowd and sing 'No Surrender' to check the whereabouts and numbers of other uncompromisers around them. It is as if the England crowd only exists as backdrop for them, just as it does for the England players. And if the rest of the English are only there as a background, the Japanese don't exist at all. A Japanese man and his son come down the steps, and with a characteristic Japanese hand gesture of a chopping wave of the palm and an inaudible 'excuse me' he tries to get past. The big boy does not even notice him, and the Japanese man with his son behind him crouches and bends double until he is but a third of the size of the Englishman, and like this he edges past.

Japan is not a place to be big. Although the Japanese are small in stature the culture makes them smaller still. On the trains there is a poster of a man seated selfishly with his legs astride and his arms draped on the backs of the seat to either side of him. He has an exclamation mark hanging suggestively between his legs and the exhortation not to take up space. Personal space in Japan is the same as personal noise: very limited in its extent. Japanese football supporters have to take a machine to matches to make themselves heard. It is an ingenious device, but all Japanese devices are ingenious: a megaphone to amplify their voices which splits down the middle to form a clapper to increase the power of their hands. But, like a hearing aid, its function is to enhance a weakness and not maximise a strength.

So our bigness and our loudness stand out in Japan, and we are the object of nervous fascination when we leave the game. They use lights to watch us in the darkness, powerful lights which emanate from police cameras and television crews. We have decided to walk to the nearest subway station rather than take the bus, but it is no stroll through the rice paddies. Instead we are herded into a channel of high wooden fences which separates us from the Swedes and which quickly becomes a dense, slow-moving river of English humanity. Police on platforms shout at us in Japanese through loudhailers, journalists and cameramen perch on the fences scanning the stream of faces for the enraged grimace of the potential hooligan. The river surges and halts annoyingly and inexplicably, and the mood after this drawn game is depressed and uncertain.

After 15 minutes we come to the explanation for the stop and surge. There is a traffic light shining out of the darkness to control the human traffic. Enforced by lines of police, when it signals red the Swedes and the Japanese from the Swedish end cross our path to good-natured booing, and then laughter at the ridiculousness of the arrangement.

A recorded message booms out. 'Please obey police instructions. Your cooperation is requested.'

'Well, you're not fucking getting it,' comes the English response. But they do get it because there is nowhere else to go. Glimpses from behind the barricades show nothing but countryside and small lanes through fields along which a few English who have escaped this confinement can be seen.

As we get closer to the station the barricades dwindle and the cordon is enforced by lines of callow, often bespectacled policemen. None of them look like any match for a belligerent Brit, but it is their vast combined presence that contains us, that and our cautiousness about how they will respond. The police and the authorities are not intimidating but neither are they intimidated. Even in the station, when a large crowd of fans without rail tickets builds up behind the

KICKING

17

ticket machines, no one tries to jump the barriers. As an experiment, and to avoid the queues, I try to pass through with the single ticket that had got me here, but, despite the crush and the presence of hundreds of the most feared fans in the world, the young guard calmly waves me back. Nobody was getting through without a valid ticket. It was the first indication that the Japanese were going to be firm in the imposition of their rules.

We are all waiting, the Japanese and the English, for something that will allow us to define the atmosphere of this World Cup. The draw against Sweden has given us nothing to celebrate and nothing to worry about. After all the anticipation and excitement of our arrival, this first game has left us in limbo until we play Argentina in five days' time. We know now we are on the train that we will be absorbed by Tokyo. This interminable city will suck us into itself and distribute us through its thousand areas and with no central point to attract us there will be no more common experiences that night.

'Sapporo will be better,' says someone beside me on the train. 'We can gather there and have a bit of a sing-song.'

No one is singing. Further up the carriage there is an Englishman with one expensive-looking shoe on his foot and the other lying mud-caked on the floor next to him. His sharply pressed jeans are also splattered with muck. But apart from this he is immaculate in a Burberry shirt. I wonder vaguely how he does it, his clothes crushed into a holdall, no irons in the hotel room.

'What's that smell?' a girl asks giggling and fanning her nose.

'What happened to your shoe?' my friend Rob asks.

Burberry's mate, who is laughing all the time, but not genuinely any more because he has laughed too much, explains that he had jumped over the fence for a piss and found himself ankle-deep in pig shit.

People laugh.

'Don't laugh,' says pig shoe, 'it's not that fucking funny.'

The aggression and pride are unmistakable in his voice, and he looks with contempt over the crumpled T-shirts, creased trousers and cheap trainers of his audience.

'They were fucking Lacoste,' he says, 'and now they're ruined.'

I arrange to meet Rob and his mates later in Ikebukuro but go on to Roppongi, the nightlife district of Tokyo and one of the urban myths that actually exists. As you come up from the subway onto the street an overpass rumbles and shrieks with traffic from the road that spans the air above. Japanese letters etched in neon throb in turrets on every building; black American bouncers thrust bills advertising sex-services towards every passer-by; call girls call. There are piles of rubbish everywhere, the roads are cordoned off by the police, and the pavements are packed with dozens of nationalities and races: Africans leaning bored and listless on the railings; Irish creating their own atmosphere; English looking for one that isn't there.

'Look at him, look at him, what the fuck's he doing in that?' This is a Scouse with a head so lacking in flesh that you can see the shape of his skull. He is pointing at another Englishman in great baggy white shorts who shrugs and walks off.

'They told me this would be brilliant. Go to Roppongi, they said, and it's all right, it's not bad, but it's not brilliant, is it?'

Two women who from their looks and accents are Eastern European, who from their clothes and body language are working in the sex trade, stagger past, one hopelessly drunk and hopeless in her sadness trying to explain something urgently to the other.

'Russians?' asks the skull-Scouse of no one. 'How much for a suck and a fuck?'

'We're going home now,' says the coherent Russian. 'Nice to meet you, bye bye.'

On the crossroads beneath the overpass there is something between a confrontation and an exchange between a small bearded Swede in full-horned Viking costume and a big Englishman with a Burberry cap.

The Swede is explaining, 'It is fun. We have all come for fun, a big party.'

The capped Englishman says something that is lost in the groan of the traffic from the roadway above, but those English who have heard him laugh. If it was funny, the situation does not look like fun, except that it is a Viking who is pleading for peace.

Further up the road there is the sound of singing. On the steps above the subterranean pub Paddy Foley's a crowd of Irish joined by a few Japanese have formed themselves into a choir. They are being videoed and photographed by dozens of Japanese pressmen. The police have pressed forward into a line to keep the pavement clear in order to prevent any pedestrians having to step out onto the road, and when any of the Irish encroach onto the pavement they are gently asked to move away. Every so often one of the Irish will detach himself from the choir and promote himself to conductor; at one stage there were three of them simultaneously directing the singing. But every time the police would move them back. On the road a second line of police are holding up notices in English. They have been printed onto sheets of paper and inserted into plastic wallets and they say 'PLEASE MOVE, BE QUIET.'

Next to me is a Japanese photographer of about 40 whose skin even in the darkness seems to glow with health. Most Japanese men of that age with all their smoking and overwork have the skin of the deceased. He looks like a typical Japanese tourist except for a telltale earpiece.

'I am a police photographer,' he explains. 'Singing, chanting OK, but we must keep the path open.' And then he says without irony, because he would not realise what he was saying, 'We want no trouble'; the incantation of everyone who has ever encountered that element of the English.

He is short and padded with a friendly open face, and two or three times he puts his arm around me in a way that is screamingly un-Japanese.

'*Many foreigners yeah*,' says a young Japanese coming out of the subway as I go back in, as if he is surprised to find so many foreigners in Roppongi during the World Cup.

As I am hesitating in the subway staring at the ticket machine trying to work out how much I should pay, a Japanese woman approaches me.

'Can I help you?'

'Thank you, I want to go to Ikebukuro.'

'This is how much. I am going that way. You can come with me.'

She is probably between 30 and 40, this woman, conventionally dressed, and though she has a ready smile, she has awful teeth, yellow and gunged up.

'Which country?'

'England.'

'Why have you come to Japan?'

'For the World Cup.'

She hesitates and giggles.

'Are you *fooligan*?'

This is the question that is being asked of the English all over Tokyo that night. The Japanese cannot help themselves. They have heard so much about the English fooligan. And the English are quickly discovering that it does not matter how you answer the question, because fooligan has become almost a synonym for an England fan.

'Of course,' I say, 'all English are fooligans.'

'Really?'

'Yes.'

On the train she tells me that it was her first time in Roppongi, that her friend had advised her that it was never busy on a Sunday night, and that her surprise was considerable to see so many foreigners. She had come to Roppongi to go to an American conversation club.

I had thought it would be a quick chat before we reached the station where we would change but it seems to be taking much longer to get back than it had taken on the way there.

I ask her where she is going and she reacts as if I have propositioned her.

'Home,' she says covering her mouth. You awful cheeky man.

Eventually we change trains and the game she is on is up. She reads the timetable in front of me, assuming that it is beyond my understanding

'You can take this train,' she says, pointing at the last one on the timetable, but even I can tell that there are three more trains before it.

'Couldn't I just take this one?' I say, pointing to one of the earlier trains.

'Yes, this one is OK too.'

'Thank you very much. Bye bye.'

I walk quickly away from her. She wants a foreign boyfriend so desperately that she has taken me far out of my way and is lying to me about the time of the train just so she can spend more time with me. She had so much love to give and no one to give it to. For somebody she would be a gift horse, but I looked her in the mouth.

At Bobby's Bar in Ikebukuro the Irish are leaving as I arrive, they think the English there are spoiling for a fight. Everyone is drunk and the tiny bar is hot with sweat and smoke. There is no karaoke but we sing 'Wonderwall', and a girl called Tina who has nothing on above the waist except a Union Jack bikini sings 'It's Got to be Perfect'. 'Tina, Ti-na, Ti-na,' the half-dozen leery men at the bar chant. There are no Japanese. Rob sings 'Anarchy in the UK' and seeing the line about the IRA coming up he makes a good fist of pretending not to notice its implications for the few Irish who are left in the bar.

A young fresh-faced lad explains his feelings for Japanese girls.

'They're so . . .' he looks for the word '. . . feminine. Tina,' he says and shrugs, 'she's not feminine with her tits and her beer bottle. Japanese girls, you could bounce a penny off their arses they're so tight, even the 30 to 40 year olds. No tits though.'

'No, they're not big on tits.'

'Even so.'

This is what it will be like all over Tokyo. Hundreds of small bars are playing host to thousands of English who are still unsure what it is that is going to characterise their presence at this World Cup. But slowly, and even while they complain about the lack of bars with televisions and the absence of open-air venues where they can watch the games, and the lack of atmosphere, Japan is starting to get them. And they do not even know it.

....

I should have known it, however. Because this was not my first time in Japan. I had spent two years there in the early 1990s, but in the ten years that had passed before I went back for the World Cup I had allowed myself to forget all about the slow burn of Japanese charm. Like almost everyone else, I thought it would be a disaster for the mutual reputations of Japan and England.

The 2002 World Cup was an important event for both countries and for the relationship between them. To the English, the Japanese were already the most nerdy of peoples. They take photos like train spotters, are swots at maths and sciences, have the interest in gadgetry and computer games of the social inadequate, and the taste in porn of the sexually depraved. They showed the bespectacled evil of the inadequate bully during the Second World War, only to replace it with the self-effacing appeasement of the timeserving company man when they lost. Their famous arts – tea ceremony, flower arranging, garden and house design, their subtle cuisine – are the province of the effete aesthete. And they have that last great

KICKING

refuge of the Walter Mitty fantasist: expertise in the martial arts.

Unlike the South Koreans, for whom the World Cup was an opportunity to show themselves almost for the first time to the world, the danger for the Japanese was that all it would do would be to increase the negativity of their nerdish image, in two ways. First, that they would, like the shy host at a party, concentrate too much on organisation and forget about the creation of atmosphere, and in the first few days this was what seemed to be happening. Their second problem was the fooligan. If they failed to show that they could distinguish between boisterousness and a serious intention towards disorder, and their lack of experience with football crowds did suggest that this might be possible, then they might over-react to one or under-react to the other, so creating a public-order disaster which would never be forgotten.

Of course, the fooligan was England's problem too. In Japan, England has always been the gentleman country, but during the lead up to the World Cup this image had come close to being broken. Primed by the media, the whole country had riot-geared itself up to meet the fooligans. Almost any act of disorder that could be described as hooliganism might destroy England's positive gentleman image in Japan, perhaps forever.

So there was much at stake, and although in the five days between the Swedish game and our date with the Argentines nothing much seemed to be happening, beneath the seeming dullness of a World Cup that had not been embraced by its host, something other than disaster was taking shape. It was missed because it had nothing to do with the World Cup. It was just the Japanese being themselves.

....

I am in a coffee shop in Kawagoe City, only an hour down the line from Tokyo, where the names of the stations seem to mock the uniformity of the suburban hinterland: South Big Tomb; Narrow Mountain City; New Place Stream; East Village Mountain; Rice River; Small Plateau; Flower Small Gold; Up Stone God Well.

It is the day after the Sweden game, and I am waiting to meet a family I do not know who have agreed to put me up whenever I am in Tokyo during the tournament. Across the road Japanese school kids, the most beautiful children in the world, are having their spirits broken by cram school. The coffee shop is dirty and a horror from the 1970s. It has fake marble-topped tables on coned bases from the 1960s. There are chairs upholstered in green plastic with turned legs and arms, and a dirty beige lino. It is the sort of dirty opulence that only the Orientals specialise in. The walls are tongue and groove, it has a mustard ceiling, and the toilet is filled with foam. The coffee is stale, and the upkeep of the premises would suggest in England that the coffee ought to cost less than fifty pence, but here it costs four times that amount. But just as I get annoyed with myself for choosing it and at the proprietor for running it, she gives me, free of charge and without my bidding, a cup of hot green seaweed soup which is delicious, and in that moment I remembered everything about how the Japanese get you. You accept the unacceptable because everybody is so kind and considerate and accommodating that you have no reasonable option but to be the same.

The family, who are friends of an acquaintance of mine, are called the Kawames, a Mr and Mrs, a lad of 16 and a girl of 13, and the first thing they do when we get back to their home late that night is to give me a key.

'*Please get up whenever you want,*' Mrs K says while Mr K draws me a map on which he includes every restaurant in a one-kilometre radius so that I might have a choice for lunch the following day.

'*We will all be out, but please help yourself to anything and please use any of the appliances.*'

I am a *gaijin* (an outside person), an England supporter and potential fooligan whom they don't know from Saddam, and they are giving me the key to their home.

'*Please use this room.*'

They open two sliding wooden doors off the main living area and show me a small six-mat *tatami* room with a futon already laid out and made up for me. Tatami are tightly woven deep rice-straw mats of a regular size which dictate the size of traditional Japanese rooms. In fact they dictate the size of everything in the house. They also determine the decor which has a strong tendency towards shades of rice-straw matting. For some people, tatami also have more subtle powers. Some Western commentators claim that the reason the Japanese are so selfless is because they don't have their own rooms, the tatami rooms being used for different purposes at different times of the day by different members of the family, so that Japanese people never develop a concept of personal space. This may have been true 50 years ago, but as I was to discover I was the only person in the house sleeping on a futon on rice-straw matting, and I was without doubt the most selfish person there. The Kawames all used beds, and the children's rooms were as postered up as any Western kid's would be. So this tatami room was a relic. It was only there because they were Japanese and being Japanese means you have to have a tatami room, much as English houses have front gardens because that's what being English means.

'Swedish style,' explained Mr K, who worked in Tokyo as an architectural consultant. Brick built, the house stood back from the road and had a forecourt with space for two cars. The entrance was up some external wooden stairs shaded with bamboo screens, and from here you went up a wide wooden stairwell into the open-plan living space. This was a big area of polished wood with a kitchen, the children's bedrooms, the toilet, bathroom and tatami room all off to one side.

It was an attractive house and reminded me that the Japanese are rightly famed for the proportions of their living spaces. They make up for their preternatural abilities in this area, however, by being completely useless at finding furniture to fit in. And the Kawames were not an exception. Every Japanese house I have ever been to has had furniture out of all proportion to the size of the rooms. They tended to favour a quasi-Edwardian style: bureaux, grand pianos, huge sideboards, tall glass-fronted display cabinets, and in the tatami rooms vast wooden chandeliers that would have been fashionable about the time electricity was introduced into Japan and which no one has since bothered to change. The Kawames had examples of them all.

The family lived mainly on this first floor and there was a separate apartment for Mr K's parents on the ground floor. I do not know if the Kawames were a typical Japanese family but typically a Japanese family would include the husband's parents living close by, so whatever the individual circumstances that had produced this arrangement it did conform to expectation. In Japan there is a saying that the ideal distance between the different generations of a family was the distance it takes for a bowl of soup to remain hot. Of course, it is very much the same in the UK, except we tend to measure the distance with the soup in a thermos flask, whereas I suspect the Japanese measure it with an open bowl. The Kawames senior were downstairs, a distance that precluded any possibility of the soup cooling.

They introduced me to the Kawames senior the following night, but when I got up that first morning there was no one in the house. They had left me to their own devices, which included a coffee machine, a toaster, a computer connected to the Internet and an air conditioner, and I made use of all four. Afterwards I went out onto the balcony to smoke and think stupid thoughts about how much closer the Japanese are to nature than we are.

Japanese balconies, and nearly all houses and apartments have them, are another relic of the old Japan, a hangover from the time when Japanese houses had a veranda running along one side. Ever since Japan was opened up to the West 150 years ago, architects have been going ape for Japanese house design, and the veranda was one of the things they fell hardest for. It had sliding doors on both the house and garden side so it could be sealed off from either, or opened to both. Western architects loved the way that the division between inside and outside, between private and public space, was not marked with boundaries and buttressed by walls as it is in the West, but was permeable, each element merging into the other without obvious division: the street into the house, the house into the garden, the garden into the landscape. The other key element in their theory was the *genkan*.

The genkan is the stone area just inside the front door where you take your shoes off before stepping up onto the wooden floor of the house proper. The genkan is conceptually public space within the interior of the house. People visiting Japanese houses will usually knock, slide the almost always unlocked door open and then call from the genkan to announce their presence. So the genkan is a little bit of public space that the Japanese have stolen and held inside their houses – much like the gas and electric meters in the West (although you rarely hear architects rhapsodising about them).

Unfortunately, the rhapsodising architects had not lived in Japan so didn't know that the Japanese mark these divisions far more rigidly than we do in the West. The difference is the Japanese do it with language.

They have different words for son and daughter, husband and wife depending on whether they are referring to their own family or another family. In fact they have a whole series of verbal distinctions to mark off the boundary between the group they are in and the rest of the world. This means that the conceptual space around the family and other groups is extremely rigid, and you know exactly where the boundaries between you and other people are, boundaries that are very difficult to cross. They are very conscious of where a conceptual space begins and ends, and can therefore be relaxed about drawing a line in the sand between private space and public space, and between outside and inside. The lines are hardwired into their heads, so much so that they don't need to be drawn in the real world at all. Solid boundaries are much more important for us because we are much freer about who is in our group and who isn't, which explains our need for low walls and privet hedges, French windows and solid front doors.

So the house I was in seemed to me more cut off from the world around it than it would in England, and its effect on me was to push me even further away from the World Cup. It was almost as if it was happening in another country. I got my information on it through the net, and the Kawames were kind enough to let me watch the games as we ate together in the evenings. And they did seem to be interested, particularly Mr K and his son. But there was none of the atmosphere either in the house or in streets or in the restaurants I visited that there had been tangible in England during Euro '96 when the tournament was all that anyone talked about. If there was any conduit connecting the Kawames and Kawagoe City to the World Cup that was being played in the country, then that conduit was me.

That day I went back to the station near Saitama stadium to see if the presence of Japanese supporters would make any difference to how I felt about Japan's lack of excitement about the World Cup. They were playing Belgium, and to get there I had to change not only trains but also stations by walking a short distance across Kawagoe City, a normal arrangement in Japan, and Mr K had drawn another map to help me. But I was confused as I left the first station so I asked a young man in a beige suit for help.

'Excuse me, I go to Kawagoe station.'

'No problem, I'm going that way too. Why don't we go together?'

He marches off confidently in what I know is the wrong direction.

'I have map, but . . .'

But . . . is a very useful word in Japanese as it suggests that there is more to what you are saying, but that you wouldn't be so rude as to state it directly. In my case what I was hoping was that he would infer the opposite of what I hadn't said *'. . . but I wouldn't be so rude as to suggest that you needed to look at it.'* The implied ending was doubly useful because there was no way that I could have put this sentence together in Japanese.

He ignores the map and continues to walk in the wrong direction. And once more Japan gets me. In England I could have done many things, my choice dependent on my temperament and my mood. I could have walked the right way and forgotten about him, or shouted after him, 'I'm pretty sure it's this way', or even 'That's the wrong way you stupid bugger'. But in Japan I have only one option: to follow him. I know that I am obligated to him for his kindness and if I were to suggest that he didn't know what he was doing, me a gaijin, he would lose face and I would betray the kindness he was showing to me.

As we are putting more distance between us and our destination, we chat.

'Which country are you from?'

'England.'

'Ah, England has a very strong soccer team.'

'Thank you.'

'What are you doing in Kawagoe City?'

And then I say a sentence that has probably never been said before in either English or Japanese.

'I want to see the Belgians. What are you doing in Kawagoe City?'

'I am a computer salesman and I am visiting some of my customers. This is my first time here.'

'Really?'

I am certain he will ask someone eventually because it is clear that he has no idea where he is going. We go about 200 yards before he finally admits to himself that he is not going to find the station by walking randomly through the city. Thankfully the person he asks isn't a stranger, because if he were then that person would then be obliged to pretend that he knew the city and there would be three of us heading in the wrong direction. So we head back the way we have come. This has cost me 200 yards in the hot sunshine, but I have saved his face, and he may never know it.

'*What country?*' asks the ticket collector at the station near the stadium.

'*England, but I want to see the Belgians.*'

But there are hardly any Belgians there, just three very affable software engineers.

I chat with them for about half an hour. Decent men in their 30s, unmarried, they like Japan, but don't like the fact that they can't find anywhere to watch the football. I ask them about the English. They have a theory. Everyone has a theory.

'What can I say,' says the Belgian in perfect English. 'What can I say about the English? Their beer you know is very weak, and then they come to Europe and drink our lager and then they get too drunk.'

He shrugs, though it is very adroit to turn our weakness for hooliganism, one of our national strengths, into a weakness for strong beer.

The Japanese supporters, and the station is streaming with them, are like the English in that they don't favour dressing in anything more than the team colours. The odd comedy supporter goes by in a samurai topknot, but en masse they prefer a simple display of patriotism rather than looking like cartoon icons from their country's past. But there is no chanting, no uncontainable anticipation being vented.

'It is like they are going to the theatre, or something,' says a middle-aged Canadian who lives in Japan and who is waiting in the queues for the buses to the stadium. 'They are so quiet.'

'If you want noise,' says a younger one, 'go to the nightclubs in Roppongi.'

There is another Canadian handing out cards with a mobile number on them and the words 'Buy Sell Tickets' in English and Japanese.

I ask him if he has had any trouble from the police.

'No, not from the police, but I was outside the entrance to the stadium and the *yakuza* moved me on.'

The yakuza are the Japanese mafia and attract the tiny proportion of Japanese people who don't enjoy helping strangers. He is slight and small and as laid-back as any Canadian. He does not look like he would trouble the yakuza.

'Was it subtle?' I ask.

'No, it wasn't subtle.'

'What did they do?'

'There was some pushing, some punching.'

'No uncertain terms then?'

'No.'

So, even though touting is illegal, he has moved to the station where there were police to protect him.

In Japan it is easy to tell if someone is on the straight and narrow: you count their fingers. The yakuza are famous for removing the fingers of those of their membership who make mistakes. The clumsy criminal becomes ham-fisted. It is the equivalent of the UK's penalty points on the driving licence, except that the yakuza only take off one at a time and when you get up to eight you are permanently disqualified from driving.

The existence of an easily identifiable criminal class also demonstrates the digital attitude to life of the Japanese. They are not an analogue people: you are either in one group or another, a law-abiding citizen or a criminal. Instead of the slow movement from member of the moral majority through the black economy through petty criminality to crime lord as there is in the UK, the Japanese divide themselves neatly down the middle of the continuum and drift quickly towards the ends. The vast majority of Japanese are in the former category, and a very few are in the latter, but each category tends to conform explicitly to type. The criminals are very vicious and the law-abiders are very dull.

Back at the Kawames I watch the Japan v. Belgium game with their son, Tatsuya. He is 16; I feel he should be gripped by it. But he does not really seem to follow the game. In fact he is more interested in supporting Germany against Ireland the next day than he is in the Japan game. His mobile keeps ringing with the jangle of a Bakelite phone on the soundtrack of a noir movie, and he misses most of the misses. It is only the goals he is interested in.

Over dinner we discuss the Belgians.

'*What is Belgium famous for?*' asks Mrs K.

'*I don't know.*'

'*Chocolate,*' says Tatsuya confidently.

'*That's Switzerland.*'

'*Belgium too,*' I contribute, and for the first time my contribution to that evening's conversation isn't limited by my Japanese, but by the fact that I know nothing more about Belgium.

We hear the news that Costa Rica have beaten China 2–0.

'Where is Costa Rica?'

'I don't know.'

We agree on Central America.

Then Arsène Wenger appears on television. He was a manager in Japan. But as he does not speak in Japanese I am assuming he was chosen because he is a known face here.

'Russia is a technical team,' he says.

There is a translation.

'They put together some good combinations.'

More translation. Then after a couple more sentences he ends with: 'Short movements round the box will be very difficult for the Russians.'

Then on the news I hear that a 34-year-old Canadian was arrested at a station near the stadium for touting. So the police were not protecting him after all.

'There are many yakuza around the grounds,' agrees Mr K when I tell him what the tout told me. *'You didn't buy a ticket, did you?'*

'No,' I say, *'very bad.'*

And I wonder briefly if the yakuza tipped the police off.

'So you are going to Sapporo tomorrow?' asks Mr K. *'Be careful. It's very dangerous, the most dangerous match of the whole World Cup.'*

SAPPORO

Argentina 0 England 1
6–8 June

IT IS ONLY WHEN YOU TRAVEL IN JAPAN THAT YOU BEGIN TO realise how huge this country is. Imagine Britain displaced and stretched out to cover France and Spain so that the West Country plunged down towards north Africa, the Channel Islands ending up on the latitude of the Canaries, with the tip of Scotland and the Orkneys level with the north of France. By going from Tokyo to Sapporo, I and hundreds of other little Englanders were going to travel the equivalent of Gibraltar to Toulouse in one day.

It was possible to get a plane, and some of the brighter or less romantic fans had got hold of some cheap offers and would fly up in an hour, but I had thought it would be more interesting to take the 12-hour train journey. So at 7 a.m. on the day before the match with Argentina, I was given a lift by Mr K to the nearest station that connected with the northward bound *shinkansen*.

The shinkansen are the famous bullet trains. They do not travel as fast as a speeding bullet; they only seem to. I was once in a station when one passed through without stopping, and, although it had slowed down to go through the station, the train still came towards me at a speed which my biology had not equipped me to handle and which it would never allow me to forget. The early shinkansen were nosed like bullets and the nickname was not one that any train system would willingly shrug off. Later shinkansen adopted a more nose-to-the-ground profile and this line of development continued until the most modern began to look like Dachshunds. Nobody calls them sausage-dog trains.

KICKING

33

The shinkansen are a train system within a train system, the elite of Japan Railways (JR). They have separate entrances within JR stations, so to get to them you pass through two sets of ticket barriers. It is like going into the inner sanctum of Japanese efficiency. Electronic noticeboards in English and Japanese tell you everything about the train, the kiosks are neater and seem only to stock an authorised range of products, the announcements are quieter and more measured, and there are elevators rather than stairs to take you up to the tracks.

You could pick anything you wished to demonstrate how much better the shinkansen are than British trains: the punctuality, the cleanliness, the reservation system, the fact that you don't have to make a will before you travel. But for me it is a very small thing. It is the way that on the escalators up to the shinkansen platforms the handrails keep pace with the moving steps. On the London Underground the handrail and the stairs move at different speeds so you are forced to keep adjusting your grip, or adopt an undignified and constantly elongating leaning stance in your attempt to keep your hands in touch with your feet. I had assumed that keeping the handrail and the stairs in synch was some impossibility forbidden by the way the universe developed in the tiniest slithers of time after the big bang. If it was, then the Japanese have found a way round it.

The reason you go up to the tracks is because the shinkansen are physically as well as metaphorically on a higher level than all other transport systems. Instead of taking the risk of cars and other trains crossing the lines, they put the shinkansen tracks on concrete stilts and in doing so created one of the defining images of modern Japan: silver horizontal streaks of lightning crossing the green rice paddies on the valley floors.

The only thing about the shinkansen that doesn't work is the uniform architecture of the parochial stations. The terminals are never seen because they are located in some of the most built-up cities in the world. But in the smaller towns the shinkansen station is like an aerodrome on the horizon: utterly pragmatic, a great sleeve of painted metal built over the tracks, completely without appeal.

So it is on the shinkansen that I begin the great journey up and down Japan: first to Sapporo in the far north and then down to Osaka, south of Tokyo, for the final group game against Nigeria. And then, should we qualify for the second round, either further south to Oita or

KICKING

34

north once more to Niigata. It will be at least ten days before I return to Tokyo.

At the station where I join the shinkansen I wait in line on the platform for the smoking carriage. Along the platform are signs to tell you which carriage is smoking and which are reserved, and lines on the platform to show you where to queue. The shinkansen always arrive with the doors aligned to the queues and always precisely on time. As it pulls in I see the front of the train is full of English, but I cannot believe my luck that there are spare seats on the carriage I am queuing for. I am so disbelieving that I ask the Japanese man next to me if this is the right train (even though one half of it is completely packed with English fans). He tells me that the train will split in half further up the line with only the front half going on towards Sapporo, and I am reassured. Like the man in Kawagoe City, he has almost certainly got it wrong.

Even Tokyo's suburbs do not go on forever, and within half an hour we are in the classic Japanese landscape of the north: plains of rice paddies dotted with houses, the tiles shining in the morning sun, the light-green grid of the rice-paddied plain contrasting with the dark-green jagged line of the mountainous and wooded horizon.

The man I had asked for advice gets off early and, having listened in Japanese to the same announcement I had listened to in English, that the whole of the train is heading towards Sapporo, he waves his reassurance. If he has been discomfited by the inaccurate advice he gave me he doesn't look it, and of course I will not make him lose face.

I have brought Basho to read on the train. Basho was a wandering poet who travelled up and down seventeenth-century Japan writing prose notes and poems inspired by what he saw. The shinkansen toward Sapporo is following in the tracks of his most famous work: 'The Narrow Road to the Deep North'. Basho, however, went nowhere near as deep north as we are going, which 300 years ago was impenetrable forest, so I am trying to read the relevant sections as we travel past the countryside he did describe. Basho of course was walking along dirt tracks, and I am travelling at 200 miles an hour on the best train system in the world so I have to read very quickly. Luckily the literary form in which Basho wrote was the haiku: the 17-syllable verse form that is one of the shortest in the world, shorter even

KICKING

35

than limericks and much less fun. So I am able to cover Basho's long journey in just over an hour and a half.

Back in the days of the first wave of HIV awareness, there was a rash of analogies about the decrease in pleasure when having sex using condoms. It was, they said, like eating a Mars bar with the wrapper on. But what sex with a condom is most like is reading poetry in translation. You get some sense of what it is all about, and it is certainly worth the effort, but you know the pleasure could be far greater. Reading haiku in translation is the absolute demonstration of this.

There are two English haiku that are any good. The first is this:

> to write a poem (5)
> in seventeen syllables (7)
> is very diffic' (5)

This is the second:

> some people are on the pitch (7)
> they think it's all over (6)
> it is now (3)

This is poetry to the English, but the odd thing about it is that it is also poetry for the Japanese, who would recognise that the simple but deeply resonant declarative sentences, spontaneous composition, internal tensions and extreme shortness are exactly what constitute a haiku. And although, its author, Kenneth Wolstenholme, uses a daring seven-six-three 16-syllable formation, it is the nearest thing in English to a genuine haiku.

What is so impressive about this achievement is its rarity. People in football are not renowned as phrase-makers. It is a celebrated English quirk that no one who is professionally associated with football has ever contributed anything to English language culture. Players and managers either speak in a replica kit of clichés or are so media-trained in the avoidance of indiscretion that they become mendacious in their banality. This inarticulacy is so pronounced that reporters switched-on enough to be embarrassed by it have to reassure their viewers that such and such a figure is in fact very articulate off camera, a tendency which said figure then makes up for by being stubbornly

KICKING

36

inarticulate when on. Apart from one famous manager's stupid, reputation-diminishing claim that football is more important than life and death, no quality phrase-making has ever come from anyone who works for an English football club (and who does not speak English as a second language).

Then there are the commentators, the people who are paid to speak. Famously word-blind, commentators are to television pictures what playwrights are to theatre scenery: the lower the quality of the one, the higher the quality the other has to be to make up for it. Modern television pictures are so good that commentators have been forced to reach anti-Shakespearean levels of language to compensate. This must be why the only commentator who ever successfully matched words to image was from the monochrome era.

Kenneth Wolstenholme's phrasing during the last seconds of the 1966 World Cup final is so contrary to the tradition of inarticulacy in football that some football people have never been able to believe it really happened. There have long been rumours that he made his closing words up beforehand or dubbed them on afterwards. Wolstenholme always denied these rumours, but in fact both are true, although not in the way the doubters want to believe.

This is what Wolstenholme said.

> the referee looks at his watch
> any second now it will all be over
> 30 seconds by our watch
> and the Germans are going down and they can hardly get up

The referee licks his lips and lifts the whistle to his mouth. Wolstenholme says the un-immortal words . . .

> it's all over I think

. . . and that would have been that. No hat-trick for Hurst, no clincher to legitimise England's contentious third goal, and, certainly on the basis of the infelicitous phrase 'it's all over (I think)', no sports-commentating immortality for Wolstenholme.

But luckily for Hurst, England and Wolstenholme, the referee waves play on.

no it's . . .
and here comes Hurst
he's got . . .

. . . struggles Wolstenholme, and then he realises that he wasn't the
only one to misinterpret the actions of the referee. Some of the crowd
have come on to the pitch and are running towards the players in
premature celebration.

some people are on the pitch

. . . he says.

Responding later to the criticism that he had pre-scripted his
famous final words, Wolstenholme would claim that nobody could
have prepared for such a moment. But this is not quite true. For if you
examine what he says you can actually hear the phrase being worked
on. He has already refined 'any second now it will all be over' into 'it's
all over I think'.

Now he refines the phrase again. He takes the words 'it's all over I
think', and changes them around, moving the 'I think' to the front of
the phrase and changing the subject from 'I' to 'they'. Then he takes
the 'now' from the words 'any second now it will all be over', adds a
dummy subject and the copula to make it grammatical, and he has it
made.

they think it's all over
it is now

These three lines 'some people are on the pitch / they think it's all over
/ it is now' have three attributes that make them poetic. First, they
draw attention to the limited time and space in which a game of
football is played. They dramatise the moment when spectators can
enter the field of play without consequences to the virtual world of the
game. Second, they contain two statements which in English are
usually described as Zen-like. 'Some people are on the pitch' is both
an alert to the unusual and a statement of the obvious (of course some
people are on the pitch, there's a football match going on). The second
statement, 'it is now', is so simple it is worth meditating upon

indefinitely. Yet it also celebrates the fact that the game was not timed out, that England did not hang on to their 1–0 extra-time win by keeping the ball in their own half, that they won emphatically with the final kick of the game. Third, because they have made the same mistake as him, in these lines he stops commentating on the game and commentates on the behaviour of some spectators, thus bringing us all into the action.

The shinkansen, perhaps as a literary tribute to Basho and to the shortness of a haiku, only goes three-quarters of the way up the Japanese archipelago. We have come half the way in a couple of hours. The rest of the journey we will do by local express train, and it will take the rest of the day. Through this long day, the sun, which had started on the right of the tracks, moves slowly over to the far left as if the train was the finger of a vast sundial crossing the landscape.

In Japan the train timetable is the word of God, and the English, used to the vagueness of an Anglicised transport system, were learning to refer to it with the literalism of a fundamentalist. Indeed in England I had never even seen a railway timetable. Train times were given only on supplication. In Japan anyone could get a copy and they had published additional ones in English for the World Cup. If the timetable said you had four minutes to change trains you knew that would be exactly what you would get. By the end of my two years living in Japan, in the stations I knew well, I was able to change trains in less than a minute and so sometimes save half an hour from my journey. The printed timetable explains why for the Japanese a station is a place where everyone rushes, whereas for the English it is a place of romance, because you never know what might happen.

So when the shinkansen reaches its terminus, all the English rush to get a seat on the local express, either to claim their reservation, or, like me, to secure an unreserved seat. I am luckier than most because I can ask in Japanese. It is my baggage that slows me down, a small rucksack and a canvas bag full of clothes. A few of the lightly loaded speed in front of me, and I wonder how some of the English can carry so little yet look so smart with just a rucksack for their clothes. Perhaps they have native porters following behind.

But I get a seat, next to a big Chesterfield man on an organised tour who is not one of the smart dressers. He is wearing a T-shirt with the legend 'Don't mention the score'.

'It's all right,' he says of the tour, 'we have got a bloke who speaks the lingo and sorts out all the problems. We spent yesterday sightseeing in Sendai, some pretty islands. But we thought it was a boring town, until we found the red-light district.'

He checks something with another of his party who is sitting across the aisle.

'But the pro's won't do it with Westerners,' he confirms, before adding quickly, 'that's not from personal experience though.'

And he says nothing else for the rest of the journey.

Outside the landscape is changing again. Now there are abandoned rice paddies choked with scrub, and the farmsteads are ramshackle, testaments to thousands of difficult conversations.

'Father, I don't want to be rice farmer, I want to trade commodity futures in the cities.'

'But, son, who will till the land, and what are commodity futures?'

I fall asleep, and when I wake up we have to change trains again. It is a tiny station in the far north of the main island. Like Scotch Corner, its importance as a node within the transport system is out of all proportion to its size, just a few empty platforms and a tiny concourse with a couple of shops. It is also the first place in Japan where I see hundreds of English but no police. There is only a team of five or six cleaners to greet us on the platform. Usually the cleaners will bow together as the train pulls in, but they cannot stop themselves from staring at us with gaping mouths. They will certainly never have seen so many gaijin in their lives. Part of their shock will be the realisation of the consequent enormity of their task: Japanese people take their rubbish with them when they leave a train; the English use the train as a place to leave their rubbish.

I have a reserved ticket for the next train, the final third of the journey, and then as we have five minutes I go onto the concourse to buy something inedible to eat. And there on the phone is Rob, the Watford boy.

He asks why I am so casual.

'I've got a reserved ticket.'

'Nobody's taking much notice of that, you know that, don't you?'

But they are. The French probably have a word for that fear you have that your reserved seat on a train will have been usurped by another: *petite terreur*. But when I get back my seat is still not taken.

Here were hundreds of English boarding a train in the middle of nowhere, all of them desperate for seats, well aware that it was another four hours before we got into Sapporo. Many have had a few drinks to dull the tedium. There were no police and the only people standing between them and train-ticket reservation anarchy were one or two slight and youthful JR guards.

On JR trains it is the carriages and not the seats that are reserved. There are therefore none of the easily dislodged tickets pegged to the top of the seats that you see on British trains. Nobody needs to go up and down the aisles reading each of the tickets above the spare seats in the hope that the reservation was only for another portion of the journey. You either have a ticket for the reservation carriage or you join the free-for-all in the unreserved cars. The guard has a master list, and after each stop he comes through and checks that those who have come into the reserved carriage have valid tickets. When he did this in my carriage, there was no one he had to turf out.

Around me people are reading books, hooligan books with titles like *Hoolifan*, *Outlaws* and *Thump Him Roger!* about people who are proud to blag their way onto trains rather than sensibly pre-booking their reservations as we have. But in the row ahead of me there is someone who has all the dodgy hallmarks of the real thing, someone with more ink in his skin than in any of those books.

One of the pieces of advice given by the British Embassy in Tokyo's leaflet titled *A Handy Guide for England Supporters* was this: 'Tattoos may cause offence. Probably best to cover them up if you can.' I can sense that drafting this document was a difficult assignment, and the writer has made a good job of striking the right tone. But tattoos were an obvious difficulty. 'Probably best to cover them up', this would have required the man in front of me to dress in a burka. Tattoos are, of course, also a sign of criminality in England, but also of military connections, masculine entrenchment, or female emancipation. Alone they signify almost nothing, but they go with other aspects of his appearance.

He has close-cropped hair and an earring. His neck is rippled like the sleeve of a gear stick, a rubber-necker, always looking for trouble. Beneath his T-shirt, his torso too is corrugated by the overlay of fat on muscle: the fat shows that he does not care about himself, the muscle, that he could look after himself if he did not care for you.

But he is a long way into his 40s, a hoolidad, and somehow his obvious toughness looks like a burden to him now. With his tattoos and earring and allegiance to a crossed flag he looks like a pirate who knows there is no way back to a settled life for him now.

The landscape is changing once more. There is so much space between the houses, and so much green that is not the green of rice plants. High in the mountains there are even things that look like meadows, and in the valleys there are areas of wooded flatness that have never been cultivated. It is the first time I have ever seen countryside in Japan.

Again I fall asleep, and when I wake up it is cold and there is mist outside. A solitary Argentine enters the carriage to smoke. He is the first one we have seen, and we watch him intently, either surreptitiously or blatantly, depending on our style. He will have got used to the English in his carriage and they will have got used to him, but here he knows that his sudden presence may provoke. But he keeps his confidence, and slides into an empty couple of seats to smoke a cigarette with panache. His cigarette-holding hand rises lazily above his head and above the level of the seat tops, curving and graceful, like a swan.

At the longest last I have ever known the train begins to slow down for Sapporo. The weather has brightened again and the city gleams in the low evening sunshine. In the far distance, the silver tear-shaped dome of the indoor arena where we will play Argentina can be seen. With the movement of the train, it is like a vast drop of mercury gliding slowly around the edge of the city.

On the platform I meet up with Rob and his mates and we go down into the ground beneath Sapporo. Many Japanese cities have underground malls of shops and restaurants on subterranean streets that run in vertical parallel with the roads above. They will often be connected to the subway systems and to department stores and hotels which exist as major landmarks in the world above. It is therefore possible to leave the air-conditioned hotel, enter the manufactured atmosphere of the subterranean mall, cross town by subway, go up into the dead air of a shinkansen terminal, board the shinkansen which is sealed from the outside world like an aeroplane, cross the vastness of Japan, go into another subway, a near identical mall, another hotel in the same chain without ever having had sky above your head or an unpumped breeze on your face or any sense that you have moved to a different place. You could spend days doing this, acting out a sci-fi fantasy of a post-nuclear world, a world in which the effects of topography and climate on culture have been eliminated.

But when, after half an hour of walking down long shopless corridors between subway stations and through the disorientating maze of the mall, we emerge into the city, we know it is different. For even though dusk is falling and there is neon climbing every building, we don't think we are in another area of Tokyo. The air is cooler and fresher, and, instead of an endless megalopolis, we know there is countryside surrounding the city and that it has a proper centre because we saw them from the train, and it feels like a place we can understand.

We find a bar in the centre of Susukino, Sapporo's downtown area and Rob and his mates go off to find the hotel while I guard the bags. It is typically Japanese: a circle of stools around the bar, the bar-top punctuated every two places by a small cooking grill sunk into its surface on which customers can put raw meat and vegetables to sear. In the main body of the room are black lacquered tables and chairs, each table with a grill at its centre, and towards the back, on a platform raised six inches above the ground, is the tatami area with its own shoe-removing genkan. It is typically Japanese, but for two things. First, it is soon filled with English who spill onto the chair-less tatami mats where they sit sprawling or with their knees uncomfortably up against their chins as they drink and eat. Second, it has a television. It is behind the bar and tiny, but is directly in front of me with a notice saying they will show France's match against Uruguay at 8.30.

Every few seconds the English come up and ask if the seats are taken, and when I tell them yes, they ask if anyone moves to call them. Others seeing my proximity to the television ask if I know the score of matches played earlier that day or yesterday. But I cannot help them, such is the paucity of information about the World Cup in Japan.

Seated round the bar are Paul of Chelsea, and Jacqueline and Steve, a couple from London. We moan.

'There's no atmosphere,' said Steve, a Beckham tribute hair-do and small colour-shaded glasses who works in security. 'I was just talking to someone in the bogs who has come over from Korea, and he said it was brilliant over there. Huge public screens to watch the matches on and thousands of people.'

'They have taken all the plasma screens down from the bars, to stop people congregating,' Jacqueline says, who works in beauty.

She does not state it because she does not need to state it, no English person does, but what she is really talking about is hooliganism.

'They want us to spend our money, but on their terms,' adds Steve.

'But they are lovely, the people. I'll think of them differently now I've been here.'

Paul and another bloke also praise the Japanese, for their immigration policy.

'We've let more people in in the last week than they've let in in the last 50 years.'

Rob returns with his mates, two of whom he has picked up while travelling through the north of Japan in the days after the Sweden game.

'Hello, darling, I'm Gemma. You all right? How you doing then?'

She sounds like Eliza Doolittle before 'Enry 'Iggins got 'er.

Then, the next moment, she sounds like Eliza Doolittle after old two-aitch had attached her aitches.

'I'm sorry, we were talking Essex all the way here and I can't stop doing it.'

It is the whole plot of *My Fair Lady* played out in 15 seconds.

We order great tall jugs of house-beer and settle in for the night. Gemma, and her travelling companion, Ken, tell tales about their flight over on Aeroflot.

'It was a disaster,' says Gemma. 'There were some real tossers on the flight. It was full of Millwall and Bolton fans squaring up to each other. One of the Bolton boys got so drunk the stewardesses actually had to tie him down.'

'It was Aeroflot's fault,' says Ken. 'They encouraged them to drink their duty-free so they wouldn't have any problems with customs when they got to Japan. By the end of it there were at least two bleeding faces, and some poor Japanese man got punched when he just knocked into someone's drink, totally by accident. They had these bottles of duty-free vodka and just kept asking for orange juice off the stewardess to mix them with. That's what happens when you fly

Aeroflot: the plane was brand new, just out of the factory, but it was still cheap.'

'And there was that classic moment when this bloke heard somebody say cunt in front of his daughter,' adds Gemma, 'and they're squaring up to each other, and the dad says, "Don't you fucking say the word cunt in front of my fucking daughter."'

Gemma's accent drifts back into Essex in her attempt to realise the story more accurately.

The hooligan question is in the air. It is everything we do not talk about. We know that Sapporo is terrified of us, that this is the most dangerous match of the World Cup. Everyone knows it, but only Mr K would state it. These lovely people are terrified of the English, or so we have been told. They have taken all the parked cars out of Susukino because the authorities have studied hooligan behaviour and noticed that they will often trash nearby cars. So the cars had to go. A garage has removed all its models off the forecourt for the same reason. Hooligans also throw rubbish bins at one another, so all the rubbish bins have gone from the streets. This is a very contextual view of hooliganism: that it might be set off by the sight of an unattended bin or a nearby car. Restaurants and bars are being boarded up in the centre of town. There are even rumours of schools near to the stadium closing for the day, presumably in case the English, finding no cars and litter bins, take to hurling school children at the Argentines. But like the Japanese, the English cannot even say the word hooligan. They call them the tossers, the prats, the idiots, the morons.

In the background France's humiliation is playing on TV like a favourite comedy, to be glanced at a while and enjoyed before returning to beer, sizzle and chat. But even as we look around at all the happy English we are all wondering – are they here, who will it be, which one of us will transform into the hooligan? Because, for all our good humour and for all our moaning about the Japanese and the absent plasma screens, we know that neither our vitality nor the Japanese moribundity will make any difference. Only tomorrow's match and its aftermath will define our experience at the World Cup, and we are in limbo until it happens.

We stay in the bar until 11 p.m., then take the subway and a long taxi ride to the hotel that Rob has arranged. It is called Mountain Villa and when I saw it in the guide I had assumed it was a typical

Japanese business hotel, its name redolent of nature, but which, in its ferro-concrete urbanity, was unconsciously ridiculing it. But it *is* a mountain villa: a real home run by an elderly landlady who does bed and breakfast.

She looks like a grandmother out of a Japanese folk tale. She is tiny and has a blue scarf on her head, a dark-blue patterned blouse, and a dark-blue skirt covering dark-blue leggings.

She greets with a bow at the genkan.

Rob, who has good Japanese, apologises for our lateness.

'Come in,' she says. 'I have poor English.'

'*No, no,*' I say, but with the enthusiasm of too much drink I say the opposite of the compliment I had intended. '*No it is different. You have very poor English.*'

'After looking please.' Grandmother leads us through the main room which is as high and broad as a barn, and slides back the paper-screened doors which make up one wall to reveal the futons laid out on the tatami. She is trusting us with an exquisite scroll which is hanging in an alcove beside a bamboo pole which rises from floor to ceiling, and her ornaments all on the floor-level shelf: a clock, a plate, some dolls, any one of which would be worth many times more what we are paying her for the night.

'Here is room, shower, toilet over there. Here is tea, coffee. Please do yourself.'

If Rob or I had not had so much beer we might have realised that she probably does not want to stay up talking at midnight to some drunken Englishmen. But we have, and so we take her at her word and make ourselves some coffee. Then we settle into the deep armchairs around the polished wooden table.

Grandmother makes no move to usher us to bed. Instead she tells us that she lived for two months in Bath 20 years ago which accounts for her English.

The phone rings although it is past midnight.

'Must go out a moment,' she explains. 'Please wait.'

Ten minutes later she returns followed by two large middle-aged Englishmen who cannot contain their excitement at having some other people to share this experience with.

'Have you seen this fucking place? How the fuck did this get into the guide?'

They come and sit down with us.

'She's fucking brilliant this one,' says one of them of Grandmother. 'We rang her from the bar we were in and said, "Look, we're going to get the subway back now. Come and pick us up." And she did. Didn't you?'

'I'm sorry?'

'It's all right, love, doesn't matter. Just pick us up again tomorrow night. Here, look at this. You have never seen anything fucking like it.'

One of the men goes to the corner of the room and points upwards.

'That's where we're sleeping . . .'

Above him, where the double height main room becomes single height, there is something like the gallery of a medieval hall. It has a wooden railing along it and there are the ends of two beds just in view.

'. . . and this is how you get up to it.'

Built on to the side of the wall is a wooden ladder going vertically up to the gallery.

He starts to climb it.

The rungs of the ladder are tiny and narrow, they are a small Japanese footstep apart, and they stand out from the wall by only a finger's breadth. Now this Englishman is, like his mate, in his 40-ish prime. He will never have been bigger or heavier before and will never be again, and watching him on this ladder is like seeing a grown man on a child's tricycle: all knees, elbows and arse. You fear for the tricycle; you fear for its rider. On the ladder the man's huge shorts-covered English arse is swaying drunkenly ever further up into the air. It protrudes far out into the room. His arse will be pulling the ladder away from the wall with a force its builder will never have reckoned on.

Even when he gets to the top he is still not safe. The ladder ends at the level of the gallery, and to get himself off it he has to squirm over the lip of the floor, his bare legs swinging ten-foot in the air.

'Fucking hell,' he says finally standing high above us in his bedroom. 'Can you believe this?'

'I think dangerous,' says Grandmother.

'Me too.'

The two men turn out to be from Leicester and had found this place in the official England supporters' guide. When he gets down, we are shown the entry.

'How did it get in here?' he asks shaking his head. 'Nobody ever checks this stuff.'

'Please silence,' says Grandmother. 'There is one more asleep.'

'What, there's someone else here?'

The Leicester lads point to the space above our room.

'Some Swiss bloke, but he's always asleep.'

'He sleep very much.'

But we don't get much sleep. We go to bed about one, and in the morning, perhaps in revenge, Grandmother starts banging the pots in the kitchen without regard for her guests.

'Fucking hell!' one of the Leicesters shouts from the gallery, but she takes no notice.

I get up and go out to buy some cigarettes and it is only then that I realise why it is called Mountain Villa and how far from the city we are. Far below in the valley, bright in the sunshine, lies Sapporo, perhaps five miles away, the teardrop stadium glittering on the very far side of the city. We are not just on the outskirts of the city, we are as far from the city as it is possible to get. For behind the villa the mountains begin. There is only one man-made feature cut into the dense forest above us: the ski-jump from the Winter Olympics.

A wooded ravine runs down past the house towards the city and I follow it down the mountain. A woman is pouring water onto the steep wall outside her home to encourage the moss to grow. We say hello to each other. It is early, and it is like the morning of a perfect English June day: one of those days when you can actually see a point to being English.

When I get back Grandmother cooks us bacon and egg with salad and coleslaw. The Leicesters are late up and I help Grandmother by translating her English into English for them.

'You want make breakfast, ham, egg, toast?'

'Do you want some bacon and eggs with toast for breakfast?'

'Coffee please?'

'Would you like some coffee?'

'Coffee please,' one sings back.

I still do not know whether any, or all four of us, were taking the piss.

We watch the television news. An Argentine fan speaking in an American accent is worried how the all-day drinking will affect the behaviour of the supporters. An Englishman interviewed in a bar slaps his hands together with relish and says, 'Tonight – bang!' A Japanese woman sitting with a child in an attractive park is asked if she is worried about hooliganism. Calmly she replies that she is more worried about the behaviour of the Japanese who can't get tickets. Despite this, it ends with a shot of a night-time street scene in Sapporo, presumably last night. In slow motion an Englishman approaches the camera and faces it out. He brings his mouth right up to the lens and exhales. The screen mists up obscuring the image of his distorted leering features.

'They ignore the fact that everyone was having a good time yesterday at the Sapporo Beer Hall,' complains one of the Leicesters.

There are 7,000 police waiting for us in the city. To explain the necessity of their presence, the news shows pictures of a Tornado taking off during the Falklands War and of Simeone contriving to get Beckham sent off at the last World Cup. Obviously this is a simplistic treatment because they have left out Maradona and the hand of God.

By mid-morning everyone has gone out and Grandmother's friend comes round for a coffee.

'Please sit down,' says Grandmother. '*Oh, sorry, silly me, I'm speaking English, take a seat.*'

'*Are they all English then?*'

'*Yes all English.*'

'*Ah, Beckham,*' says the friend, partly for my benefit.

Grandmother tells her friend how late we come back and how we ring her from the subway station in the middle of the night to get her to pick us up.

'*It must be very hard work,*' sympathises the friend.

'*Yes, some of them understand nothing.*'

But it is not such hard work that Grandmother is not prepared to take some more in. The phone rings throughout the morning and every time she says yes, she has some space. Then she rings her daughter or daughter-in-law who lives nearby and gets her to put some of them up. By the end of the morning she has at least ten English on her hands. She comes and goes, picking some up and bringing them back up the mountain to her daughter's, more than happy to leave me alone in her house, a stranger and, according to all the TV she has seen, a potential hooligan. She is either trusting to the point of naiveté – a fooli-gran – or more wise about human nature than the media, and the longer I hear her taking bookings from the English the more I think the latter.

'Fucking dangerous,' says a voice from above.

I had forgotten about the sleeping Swiss. He turns out to be an England supporter whose English is so good he has learned the social value of saying 'fucking' in the first sentence he uses.

We chat and smoke for a while. He was at Munich when we beat the Germans 5–1 and was made just as happy as the English by the result. He smiles and laughs a lot, and his rate of saying the word 'fucking' slows as we get on. He has been doing some walking in Japan and is trying to keep it very cheap. He has even slept rough in a field near Saitama for England's game against Sweden and then the next night on an industrial site under a railway bridge. There he was woken by the work-gang who turned up early the next day, and the foreman felt so sorry for him that he was invited to spend the next night at the foreman's home. But after coffee and a couple of cigarettes, the Swiss also leaves.

Grandmother kindly offers to take me down to the subway station in her car as she has to pop into the post office. I go in with her and watch as she tries to blag a discount with an out-of-date card.

'*So sorry,*' says the clerk, '*but this card is no longer valid.*'

'*What a mistake to make, I am a very foolish old woman,*' she says or something like it, but somehow I do not think it is a mistake.

As I stroll from the subway station towards the centre of town, four Englishmen are striding away from it. From a distance I think the central older man in the group is a dad. His trousers are about three inches too short, and absent-mindedly I assume he has borrowed them and because of his age does not mind that they look ridiculous. But as they get closer I can see how wrong I have been. They are walking swiftly with purpose, almost military in their bearing. They are strung out across the streets and the half-mast man sizes me up through his light blue sunglasses as he passes me. 'Are you one of us?' his gaze asks. 'No, but I can see you know who I am now.'

I had thought them the centre of the crowd, a dark sink of power around which the rest of us orbit at whatever distance our moral strength and physical courage will allow. But in Odori Park, in the middle of Sapporo, something else was beginning to happen.

KICKING

In the daylight Sapporo feels even more like a Western city than it had at dusk the night before. The weather is warm but the sun does not burn. The streets are wide and divide the city into American-style blocks. It is nothing like the twist and swirl that is the cityscape of Tokyo. And in Odori Park there are avenues of trees, a fountain, flowerbeds, and, that most rare of Japanese floral delicacies, grass. Here the English have laid their flags, and gathered to caper and sing.

And slowly, instead of shunning us suspiciously, the Japanese begin to join in. Englishmen, who because of their forbidding appearance – the hoolidads of legend – are approached by earnest students and giggling schoolgirls with such earnest good humour that even the hardest of them could not fail to return it. Gangs of leery lads are asked to pose for photos with gaggles of cute young girls-about-town who rotate the honour of posing with the English among all their friends. Everywhere there are scenes of Anglo-Japanese mixing that none of the English, after their experience in Tokyo and their awareness of Sapporo's fear, had ever anticipated.

A Millwall fan, huge, older, intimidating in his size and his appearance, as well as his connection to that fabled fooligan club, is deep in communication, if not language, with a tiny young Japanese lad. The Millwall is explaining that he cannot eat raw fish, that he will only eat cooked meat.

'Fire, fire,' he says, 'must fire to eat.'

And the Millwall mimes lighting a fire and stoking a grill.

The student nods happily. The Millwall holds up his big chunky arms and crosses them in front of his chest. The Japanese gesture for no, forbidden.

Some Japanese schoolgirls pose for photographs with an Englishman.

'Are you Gary Glitter? Are you Gary Glitter? Are you Gary Glitter in disguise?' shouts the crowd happily.

A man strips naked and mounts the mound of pansies in the middle of the park to cheers. His thin wiry buttocks are level with the heads of the crowd. The schoolgirls cannot believe what is happening and show their excitement by jumping up and down with their fists clenched. A policeman steps over. There is a moment when we all wonder what will happen, but he stops him with just a smile and an apologetic shake of the hand. The stripper's clothes go back on.

For about half an hour the crowd plays a vast game of keepy-uppy, the ball arching high along the avenue of trees. There are great cries of 'whoa' and 'whoo' as it rises and falls. When it comes down people are selected at random out of the crowd, Japanese and English, and both join in to keep it aloft.

'Can you hear the Argies sing?' we ask.

'I can't hear a fucking thing,' we reply.

They were here earlier. Their presence can still be seen where an Argentine shirt has been left on one of the statues in the centre of the park, an England-shirted statue next to it. But if any of them remain, they have been overwhelmed by the huge English crowd.

Another Englishman mounts the pansy mound. He is balancing a Japanese girl on his shoulders, but backwards, in piggy-front style. His nose would be in her crotch but he turns his head demurely along her thigh. It is a feat of strength and balance but he gets her up there. The crowd is cheering, she is blushing and giggling. The crowd seeing her position, her youth, her nationality, shouts 'Sushi! Sushi!'

The amazing naked man, the juggling, the acrobatics: we are the circus and we have come to town.

I ask two young Japanese women if they had come here to see the other fans, the Germans and Saudis, the Italians and Ecuadorians, and what did they think.

'*This is bigger and better,*' they say.

'*Strange gaijin,*' I comment using the classic phrase the Japanese use of foreigners.

'No,' one corrects me firmly, perhaps picking up the slight criticism of the conventional Japanese response in my words, '*it is interesting.*'

I bump into the lad from the bar in Ikebukuro who had praised the penny-bouncing tightness of the Japanese female arse. He and his mate are ticket-less but happy. They slept last night in a youth hostel with 12 others, English and Argentine, all in a single room. The hostel was located beneath the railway tracks over which trains passed every few minutes, and to escape the noise they got drunk to get through the night. Now they are getting drunk on anticipation and lager, a huge case of which is on the grass ten feet away.

'I'm worried about our beers,' he says every other minute, but they stay safe on the grass. He can do nothing about them, because young and handsome as he and his mate are, every second minute a hesitant group of girls comes up to ask if they can have a picture with them.

'I never understood why famous people mind so much having their photograph taken,' he says, 'but now I do.'

But they never refuse and always agree with good grace.

The day turns to evening, but even though all the convenience stores around the park have sold out of beer, the circus-picnic atmosphere never changes. Sapporo, the city that we had been told was terrified, had welcomed us. Perhaps the Japanese came at first because they wanted to experience the frisson of the foreigner, to associate themselves with the authenticity and danger of the England brand – and some of us were literally branded with hot metal tattoos. But they stayed, and called their friends on their mobiles to join them, and pulled by their presence other strangers in, because they liked what they found. Perhaps they felt so safe in their home city that they could not believe anything could go wrong; perhaps having discovered that the English were not all fooligans they concluded that none of us were; perhaps they are just better people than anyone else who had hosted a World Cup. But with friendliness, trust and openness, the young people of Sapporo came into the swirling, combustible mass of the English and changed what we thought of them and perhaps what we thought of ourselves.

It is so pleasant in Odori Park that it is almost a shame to leave, only the match itself is a good enough reason to go.

There are free buses running from the park to the stadium, but I take the subway because I have arranged to meet Rob's gang at the stadium station.

'Have you ever seen an underground system as crap as this?' a group of English ask themselves rhetorically. 'What do they need air conditioning for? And why doesn't it stop for 20 minutes in a tunnel for no reason like they do in England? And who needs these electric signs telling you which station you're coming into? And in English too. What a waste of public money! It's too clean. There are too many cleaners. Have you ever seen a cleaner on the Underground? No, that's because they wait till we have all gone home, there's none of this cleaning the platform while there are passengers on it, getting in the way. What's your favourite Northern Line station? Morden? Balham?'

Once more, as the packed carriage of English and Japanese speeds

KICKING

smoothly towards the stadium, we ask why we can't hear the Argies sing.

'They're not on the train because they can't afford the tickets,' says one of the ironic complainers.

Then they start chanting, 'We're burning US dollars. We're burning US dollars.'

They lead us off in a chorus of 'God Save the Queen' and then get a game Japanese lad to sing 'Kimigayo', the Japanese national anthem, while the other Japanese smile mysteriously and tolerantly, but do not join in.

As I wait for Rob and his friends outside the station near the stadium, I am able to watch the English stream past. The crowd seems more varied. There are more costumes: a woman in cloak and crown; two men dressed as knights, the lad with them as a dragon. I hear deep London voices and Midland twangs, Scouser excitement and Geordie affability. There are more families, and many lads and dads, far more than I had been aware of at Saitama.

'There are more women and families than at any England game I have ever been to,' agrees Gemma when she arrives.

We stream up with the rest of the English. The stadium pushes its silver nose round the corner of the buildings like a monster shinkansen, shimmering in the last light of the evening sun. A water cannon has been parked up along the route like a display of Soviet power. The anticipation in all our minds communicates itself without words, in the body language, hurry and excited voices of everyone who congregates on the forecourt. We wait before going in. We want to enjoy this moment. We know that we are about to enter a match that will be talked about for decades, and we want to record our presence in our memories and in photographs.

Suddenly there is a commotion, and every one of the 40 or so professional cameramen on the concourse rushes to its source. An English fan has been arrested and is being bustled like a wounded American president towards the road. He is surrounded by police and by a maul of cameramen. They are a writhing mass of humanity, like hounds surrounding the body of a fox. He raises his head to say something, but the whirring and firing of the cameras obscures any sound he makes, and then a policeman's hand forces his head back down. It is like the commotion caused by a shamed celebrity or an infamous criminal, both of which he has now become.

Just after this has happened, an Englishman we do not know appears beside us, and explains that the man was drunk. Our informant is alone, and there is something that seems not unrelated about his sudden appearance among us, and his knowledge about the incident. But there are tales of undercover police spotters everywhere, and our nerves may be pitched too high.

It is dark outside by the time we enter the covered stadium. The lights, the flashes of thousands of cameras, the noise of two sets of clamorous supporters, each hating the other, and the tense expectation combine within the enclosed dome to create a sensory and emotional tension that will not be relieved by any sense of the external world for two hours. It feels this time as if we have been sealed inside World-Cup-world.

No one at the English end can hear the Argentine national anthem for they are either booing themselves or are surrounded by others booing. We sing our own of course, although Ken and Gemma, who are sitting behind me, and Rob, are singing their own words: a republican alternative for this jubilee year.

> Sven-Goran Eriksson,
> Sven-Goran Eriksson,
> Sven-Goran Eriksson,
> For President.

'I don't think people get it,' said Ken later. 'The republicanism isn't obvious enough.'

'How about losing the second Sven line and putting in "and not that German queen"?' I say. 'That might make it more punchy.'

'Hmm,' he says cautiously, 'I think that might take it too far.'

The England crowd might harbour a range of views on the constitution of the United Kingdom: from no surrender to the IRA through to its own small republican wing. But Ken, I think, realises that there is a perceivable centre and that it is long way from republicanism. He doesn't want to have too much punch.

Every time that Beckham touches the ball, the rate of flashing cameras around the ground increases in direct proportion to his fame.

Then, as he lines up to take the penalty late into the first half, the flashing reaches levels where they should warn the epileptics to look away.

When he scores, the English crowd surges back and forth as people lose their footing in their leaping excitement. The lad beside me hugs me, his arms still, and his hands in a fist, so as not to compromise the acceptable physicality of the moment with any suggestion of a finger caress.

'I recognise those tits from Tokyo,' says a man along the row from me pleasantly, as we sit down at half-time. He is looking at Gemma's breasts.

Gemma takes it happily; she has been in football crowds since she was 14.

'The Japanese can't believe them,' she says. 'It's been eyes down ever since I got here.'

'No tits in Tokyo,' muses the man, 'but there's more up here. They're bigger generally, the people.'

There are so many types of English here: hoolidads with big known faces and big bodies whose flesh if cannibalised would taste of beer, tattooist's ink and testosterone; young sharp-dressed geezers from the big city clubs; students like the lad who hugged me; ex-pats from Australia, Singapore and Hong Kong; graduate professionals like Gemma who wear their support of football without shame for their intellect or their earnings; public school boys in England rugby shirts; macho tattooed boys in their prime with well-paid manual jobs; nerdish football obsessives on whom the game confers some masculinity; English whose parents or grandparents came from the Asian sub-continent; white Asia-heads with wiry bodies and loose clothing and the arrogance of alien experience; traders and teachers, the residents of Japan who are following a World Cup for the first time; 20-somethings on a year off on their way to or from Australia; official England supporters with their talk of the failings of the bureaucracy under which they travel; and finally the biggest group, though not necessarily the majority – the club supporters with their local affiliations for clubs in the Nationwide, displayed consciously through flags and unconsciously through accent.

They are all here and they all make up the crowd, and instead of being in orbit around the hooligans, being 1–0 up to Argentina makes it feel more like a constellation of an English heaven.

For the second half, Ken has saved up a nice line in Argentine taunts.

'At least the pound's still quoted,' he shouts, and, 'You're going home on a bankrupt airline.'

With Gemma, he has created an alternative lyric to 'Don't Cry for Me Argentina'.

Start crying now Argentina,
The truth is he always misses.
He's fucking useless,
He's fucking useless.
That Batistuta,
He's a wanker.

Obviously these songs and witticisms are never going to reach the Argentines who sit in a block at the far end of the stadium. They are our contribution to the totality of the event, which isn't just about what the players get up to on the pitch.

Much of the entertainment is derived from hating the Argentines.

'You dirty Argie bastards. You dirty Argie bastards,' we shout.

But it is not real hatred; we are playing with our own emotions. Our hatred for the Argentines is as much an emotional contrivance as a Viking costume on a reasonable Swede. In World-Cup-world we are allowed to puff up our emotions until we become cartoon versions of our real selves.

'Same old Argies, always cheating,' we chant at any incident that involves an Argentine player and the referee. It reminds us of two of the three reasons why we hate them: Simeone's gamesmanship with Beckham in the last World Cup, and Maradona's cheating the ball past Shilton four World Cups ago.

It has always been assumed that Maradona's description of this incident as 'the hand of God' was prompted by self-referential vanity. But he may have seen more deeply. Football, like any game, is all about limits: limited time, delineated space, and a limited range of actions that can be performed. It allows us to see what people are like by simplifying their choices and goals. By taking something from the real world – the obvious fact that anyone can put a ball into a goal with his hand despite the name of the game – Maradona did something that

KICKING

57

was, in the prescribed world of the game, miraculous, as miraculous as a moving statue would be in normal life, something that could only be attributed to divine intervention: to the hand of God.

In art, when this happens, when the real world intrudes into the prescribed world, the effect is nearly always comic: the boom that appears in shot; the actor who forgets his lines. We laugh at the realisation that we have been taken in. But in sport the effect is tragic. By borrowing from the real world Maradona over-reached himself, and so made the Faustian pact that would eventually claim him.

But Maradona's cheating and Simeone's gamesmanship are not the only reason we loathe the Argentines, we too have borrowed something dangerous from the real world to increase the power of our experience in World-Cup-world: we have borrowed war. Undoubtedly, and, as the Japanese television report included, part of what enhances the hatred we express for the Argentines is the fact that we went to war with them. It is the same with the Germans, the only other nation that English supporters loathe so intensely. To be loathed in World-Cup-world a nation has both to be a footballing power and a recent adversary in the real world. This is our own Faustian pact, and although on this occasion it makes the relief and joy we feel at England's victory the more intense, if we had lost, we would have taken a risk that some of us would not have been able to leave our antipathy behind in the sealed stadium.

But when the whistle blows all this means nothing. We have seen England beat Argentina and now are part of English footballing history, and all we want to do is celebrate the fact.

Once again the slow progress of the march out into the darkness frustrates us. It is an easy stadium to exit, not five minutes from the subway station, but it takes an age, and the queue on the wide terrace outside the stadium stops and starts like it did in Saitama.

The reason is the same. The Japanese are letting the crowd through in pulses to stop a rush down the steps towards the road. A burly policeman with a white whipping stick held vertically above his head is muscling his way like a cavalry officer through the crowd leading a line of policeman carrying a chain.

'Who's the wanker? Who's the wanker? Who's the wanker with the stick?' the crowd chants, and I sense that the Japanese around us are becoming nervous. They are so much smaller than us, and there are a lot of women in the crowd. They cannot see what is going on ahead of them and cannot understand the chants which must sound as aggressive and anarchic as they actually are.

Finally we get through the wanker stick line and reach the steps. Here a Japanese policeman with a loudhailer is advising everyone in Japanese to move slowly and be careful as there are steps.

'*Eigo de, eigo de, eigo de hanshite!*' Rob shouts, and we join in, explaining to the English around us that it means speak in English, and the others take it up. And now the Japanese are laughing because they have understood something, not just the language but the culture of the English crowd. The Japanese have a proverb: the nail that stands out will be hammered down. It means that anyone who sticks out should be driven back into line. As for the English, we lambast anyone who gets above themselves, and lampoon anyone who sets himself above the rest of us. Stuck-up English nails are also hammered down, but with a comedy mallet.

For the first time I feel that we are doing more than just swelling the English crowd and contributing our voices. I feel that we are contributing something specific to the atmosphere.

'How do you say we love Japan?' asks Ken.

'*Nippon o daisuki.*'

'*Nippon ga daisuki,*' corrects Rob.

So to the tune of 'We Love you England', we start to sing, '*Nippon ga daisuki.*' This too is taken up and makes the Japanese happier still. They start cheering.

When we finally reach ground level we find a solitary Argentine holding a placard with an image of two hands shaking. He is clapped with hands held high, and cheered, for we are English and we are magnanimous and only a little patronising in victory. And the road to the station is lined with Japanese people who are clapping us and holding out their hands to be shaken or slapped as we pass.

Everybody is looking at each other now. There is no Tokyo pretence that we do not see each other on the subway station or on the trains. We know Sapporo is small; we know we are not going to be split up and absorbed; we know we can stay a crowd as long as any of us want to.

On the train we sing all the songs and chants, and tell the jokes we had used in the stadium: 'Sven-Goran Eriksson for President'; 'He's not Swedish Anymore'; 'You're Going Home with the French'.

'That one works,' says one critic, 'everyone hates the French.'

We are just starting to sing 'Start Crying Now Argentina' when Rob sees an English lad of not more than seven or eight standing with his parents on the packed carriage.

'Children present,' Rob warns. So we sing it with censorship.

> Start crying now Argentina,
> The truth is he always misses.
> He's effing useless,
> He's effing useless,
> That Batistuta,
> He's a double-u.

And then, hearing how we lead off with a few words which are then taken up by the others, the boy's little voice sings out 'Argentina failed', and to make him happy somehow we turn this unrhythmical snippet into another chant.

As we come up from the subway onto Sapporo's Susukino crossroads, there is a crowd of about 100 English and Japanese across the road chanting and jumping up and down with tight-packed exuberance. The police are trying to stop people crossing the road to join in. At the time I thought this was a focus of English celebration, but I soon realised exactly the same thing was happening all over Susukino and in Odori Park. All that night I thought I would make my way to the park, but some incident or spontaneous celebration would stop me, and I would postpone it for half an hour. And I kept doing this until dawn came up. The whole of that night, nobody in an England shirt ever thought the party was elsewhere.

Instead of crossing the road to join the throng we start singing across the street towards them, and like the injection of a drug, the change in this busy nightlife street is immediate. Suddenly the half dozen or so of us English are surrounded by dozens of Japanese young people who are copying us and joining in. *'Nippon! Nippon! England! England! Nippon ga daisuki!'* Flags are waved in the air above us. The crowd around us swells from 20, to 30, to 50, a few more English but mostly Japanese, and now the police are turning their attention our way.

'Look,' shouts Ken, 'when we started there were more over there, but now there are more here.'

A middle-aged man with a big, old-fashioned camera gets himself into the centre of this mêlée to photograph the gaijin, but particularly Rob: earring, short hair, ebullient, anarchistic tendencies.

The police photographer withdraws, but just after he does so a tall angry Japanese youth barges his way through to the centre of the dancing crowd. He begins to remonstrate with one of the Japanese kids who is holding on to the other end of Rob's England flag, almost certainly berating him for holding the flag of a nation other than Japan. He seems to be about to hit him for this offence, but Rob and another Englishman intervene. The tall youth then grabs the end of the England flag from the kid and tries to walk away with it, but Rob is having none of this, and neither am I. We both pull on the flag with our arms high, stretching it between us and the tall youth into a tense horizontal barber's pole of red and white. The tall youth maintains the pretence that he is just walking casually away, but he isn't moving. Eventually he lets go and stalks off muttering.

Until that moment I had always thought that, although carrying the flag to the football was acceptable or even encouraged, in some way we had appropriated it, that it was like the pound or the passports in our pockets, the property of the state, that the cross of St George existed in some vault of gold or information held by the government and was only granted to us for our use. But after that moment I saw that the England fans were the only people who used the flag properly, to do something with it that the military and the monarch no longer do: to announce and identify themselves from a distance to others, either friend or foe, and that all those England flags with Grimsby or Portsmouth written across them weren't appropriated but were the real thing. He tried to steal our flag, but we didn't let him.

Apart from this, there was only one other negative incident during the whole night, when a member of the yakuza pushed his way past as angrily and with as much muttering as the flag-napper. The yakuza probably control Susukino, but for this night they weren't in charge and evidently this wasn't making this one happy. When I say he was a member of the yakuza, I am making as many assumptions as people make when they say someone is a hooligan. Unless you see someone engaged in a hooligan act you have no way of knowing if someone is a hooligan. For me a hooligan act is defined as inflicting damage to people or, while in low spirits, to property in connection with a football loyalty. The reason I add 'while in low spirits' to my definition is because when I was younger I was always damaging property in high spirits so I had to frame a definition which excluded the possibility that I might condemn myself. As I couldn't count this yakuza candidate's fingers all I had to go on was his clothes, styling, and general demeanour. His demeanour I have already described so he was either a yakuza or a nationalist. His styling was over-styled: he had unnaturally high hair and side-burns which suggested a vanity that you do not see in the ordinary Japanese, and thirdly he was wearing a flashy cream suit which again is unusual among the Japanese.

The fact that these two tiny incidents are something to write home about shows how lacking in aggression nearly all Japanese are. I do not know how many joined in that night or who passed the English by without a problem, but these were only two people among thousands. It was impossible to tell how many, or whether any of them stayed out on the streets the whole of the night as we did. I suspect many came and went to bars, clubs and karaoke, joining in for half an hour or an hour as they made their way to and fro, but the streets were the only place to be. For the first time in Japan, the people who had managed to secure a seat in a bar weren't the lucky ones.

It was like carnival and it lasted until dawn. An inexhaustible supply of enthusiastic young Japanese danced with us, chanted with us, shook our hands and even hugged us in the tense-muscled fist-fingered manner they had learnt from the English. There were cameras flashing all around us and boys and girls in equal numbers. It was as if they had been given permission by our presence to party on the streets en masse. I had never seen anything like it before either in Japan or England.

'It was like New Year's Eve,' said an older couple later, 'New Year's Eve like it used to be, when you could go anywhere and when everybody was your friend.'

'How can anyone cause trouble now?' said one fan, 'You just couldn't do it.'

The policing was also brilliant: 'Chanting, singing OK, but we must keep the roads open.' This is what they did. On every street corner for around four blocks there would be groups of English and Japanese partying. The police, instead of standing round in groups creating a focus, looking for trouble and so creating it, spread themselves along the edges of the pavements and concentrated on keeping the crowds off the roads. They knew that if they looked like traffic cops they would not be resented, and they weren't. There was lots of chatting to them and photos taken with them. Even when the crowd would swell and burst onto the road, all the police would do would be to back away and put cones down to define the new edges of the road. The crowd would swell again and the cones would encroach further. But it wasn't deliberate, nobody was testing the police, and politely they would request the people on the edges to move back towards the pavement, and slowly, because the world was getting drunker, they would move. And if someone climbed a lamppost they would gently urge him down.

Perhaps like the Japanese who were coming and going through the night, we took a break after a couple of hours and went up into a fourth-floor restaurant.

'I am sorry,' reads a sign, 'hooligans isn't to come in.'

But Rob's Japanese convinces the bouncer we are unlikely to be hooligans.

Another sign warns against foreign payment.

'For cash,' it says, 'for the sake of promptness, summing up your orders as group is recommended (for short no Dutch treat).'

Once inside we know we have to ring Grandmother up at Mountain Villa to tell her we might be late. This is slightly disingenuous as it is already two in the morning, and neither Rob nor I like the utter contempt with which we are taking her hospitality, Japan having got us both a long time ago. Of course our guilt does not only come from her age, it comes from the fact that we wish to repay her faith in human nature, and here we are at two in the morning keeping an old woman up with every intention to keep her up much later.

We rejoin the street party an hour or so later and now the drunkenness is in full swing. The convenience stores have sold out of beer and the English are having to drink cocktails of cheap vodka and orange, or swig *sake* or whisky or *shochu* – another rice spirit – from bottles, the bottles being passed from English to Japanese and back. They are even reduced to chanting the names of the convenience stores in tribute. 'Lawson, Lawson!'

But this inebriation has not changed the atmosphere, although there is more staggering and conversation is less focused and more prone to error. I have never seen so many English people pause only to smile.

'It was like this in Munich, after we beat the Germans,' says a big Brummie, swigging sake outside a Lawson.

'Surely not with the locals?'

'No,' he concedes, 'not with the locals. They're going barmy, though, one of the kids lit a flare and ran through the off-licence. The police took him aside and when he got back to his friends he was treated like a hero.'

'They can't believe it,' says someone else of the Japanese. 'They'll go back to their little jobs in the morning with stories forever. They'll talk about it forever. We'll talk about it forever.'

Finally there is a chant for the evening which I hear on the streets and on the train the next day, and which perhaps becomes the official chant for this event.

> Hello, Hello, Hello,
> The English are in Sapporo.
> We're drinking your beer, left the Argies in tears.
> The English are in Sapporo.

And suddenly it is daylight. It was, without a shadow, one of the best nights of my life.

....

Grandmother is still up when we get back to Mountain Villa. She is looking unhappy under her blue scarf.

Three or four hours later I get up. Grandmother of course is up as well, though she seems less chilly than she was at 6 a.m. Perhaps her mood is swinging due to sleep deprivation.

I apologise and try to explain how last night was a moment that I will never forget, but it is difficult to get her to say the words I want her to say in return.

'I understand how important it was that England beat those Argentines,' I want her to say. 'I know they cheated in the 1980s and got the living god David Beckham sent off through a knavish trick during the last World Cup. It was perfectly acceptable for you to stay out until that time. In fact, I could have understood it if you wanted to stay later, and I admire your consideration for me in breaking off from the party at 5.30 and allowing me to sleep for an hour. I can only say it has been an honour for me to be in this very small way a part of this great historical occasion, and I thank the gods that I was alive to see it.'

Instead she says, 'No breakfast today.'

Also her advertised benefit of taking her guests to and from the station has been quietly put aside so I walk down to the bus-stop before Rob, the Leicesters, the sleepy Swiss, or the other English she has squirreled away appear. Whether they are even in yet I do not know.

OSAKA

Japan 1 Russia 0
Nigeria 0 England 0
8–13 June

THAT NIGHT CHANGED EVERYTHING, AND WE ALL KNEW IT. ALL the doubts we had felt about whether this World Cup would take off in Japan had gone and taken with them all our uncertainty about the Japanese. We knew that they loved us, and that we loved them.

No one who was there will ever forget it. A unique combination of factors had created a perfect moment of spontaneous carnival: an English victory over a cheating enemy; a welcome from the Sapporeans that nobody had anticipated; the climate and layout of the city itself; the intelligence of the policing. All of this had changed how we felt about the Japanese.

In the days between Saitama and Sapporo, the English had found themselves confronted by two contradictory impressions of the Japanese. On an individual level they had been the kindest and most helpful of people, but only to individual English people and to small groups. En masse their response to the England crowd had been hesitant and nervous. After Sapporo, with the official actions of the police and the participation of thousands of young Japanese, this contradiction in their behaviour had ended. They had welcomed us both as individuals and as a nation.

The train back down south next morning is deadly quiet. A lad with eyes so hooded that they should really be perched on a thick leather glove on his arm tells me it was one of the best nights of his life, then falls asleep for three hours. Up the carriage a woman spends hours doubled up and writhing in what I hope is hangover pain, while the man she is with tries to comfort her. Behind me two lads who cannot sleep quiz each other on England football facts for the whole of the first four-hour leg of the journey. By the end they are asking each other to guess the weight of England players, both individually and in combination.

Thankfully I do not have to go all the way back to Tokyo with them because I am stopping off in Sendai. If Sapporo, the northern capital, is equivalent to Edinburgh, and on a stretched and twisted England overlaid on Japan Tokyo is London, then Sendai would be the geographical equivalent of York. I am stopping there because I want to see whether the South Americans, the Mexicans and Ecuadorians, who are playing in the city the next day, will have as much as fun as we had.

It is only 40 minutes between the most northern point the shinkansen gets to and Sapporo, and I am sitting in a near deserted reserved carriage when three Englishmen come up the carriage and sit in the seats alongside me: one on the far left of one row, one in the middle of the next one, and one on the far right of each of the triple row of seats. This is an oddly regular arrangement, and it signals two things. First, that after only a week and a half in Japan, they have chosen to arrange themselves into an aesthetically pleasing staggered formation. They have placed themselves in a line and are using me as a dot to define the English space on the train, Japanese aesthetics having got them so quickly. Second, in a provocative act of English fuck-u-ism, it is obvious from their decision to sit in this arrangement that they cannot have reserved tickets.

These are big lads, all in their 30s, and one of them is wearing a Burberry shirt. Now a lot of Japanese women of a certain style wear Burberry shirts and I do not want to cast beige tartan aspersions on anyone who wears Burberry. I am not suggesting that Japanese women who wear it are hooligans, and I am not suggesting that the English men who wear it are effeminate, I am just pointing the fact out. But I would not have taken these men on either singly or in a couple, or even in the aesthetically attractive threesome into which they had arranged themselves. And I do not envy the guard who will appear any moment to discover their duplicity.

The Japanese sitting in front of them has no problems with their presence because it has just not occurred to him that anyone would dare sit in a reserved seat carriage without a reservation. He twists in his seat and chats to the lad behind him, the one with the Burberry shirt, and I am guessing, because I couldn't hear, but the conversation almost certainly went like this.

'Which country?'

'England.'

'England football team, very strong.'

Then in one of those kamikaze acts of kindness with which the English are becoming familiar, the Japanese gives his new English friend his packet of fags. The Englishman smiles with pleasure and some humility and pleads with a few words and many hand gestures that he cannot accept them; the Japanese insists, and the Englishman accepts with grace. In an attempt to return the favour he tries to give the Japanese man his own packet of cigarettes (Embassy I think, but from a distance it's hard to be accurate). But the Japanese will not allow him to do so.

Further along the carriage the pirate-hoolidad from the train up to Sapporo has also got onto the reserved smoking carriage. But he doesn't stay long. A friend comes in and must be telling him that they have got him an unreserved seat in another carriage, because sheepishly and disappointingly, he gets up and goes with him.

In the devil's catalogue of debauchery, taking a seat in a reserved carriage would not put you in hell, but I knew the Japanese guards would not tolerate it. Most Japanese people take their jobs very seriously, and they are just too diligent to ignore anything simply for the sake of a quiet life.

But because most Japanese people take rules and regulations just as seriously, the guard who is about to come and check our tickets will be used to a quiet life. Very rarely in his railway guarding life will he ever have had to deal with anyone deliberately usurping a seat in a reserved carriage. It is an act of vandalism against the transport system that is, in English terms, the equivalent of pulling the communication cord or putting obstacles on the line.

The guard appears at the end of the carriage and starts to check tickets. The English lads verbally nudge one another. The Burberry shirt at the front pretends to go to sleep, the one in the middle folds his arms and the one at the back reads more deeply into his paper. The guard, this guardian of correct procedure, is a small, slightly fat man.

This is not going to be a battle of physical presence. It is going to be a clash between the belligerent freeloading ghost of the English and the Japanese machine.

The automatic announcement comes on. 'This train will soon be making a brief stop in Sendai . . .' and I worry that I might miss the outcome.

But he is swift, this guard, and he gets to the one in front before the shinkansen slows down for Sendai. The one in front's strategy is to pretend to be asleep, but the guard is not to be discouraged. He leans into the Englishman's space and the Englishman pretends to wake up.

'Well, that didn't work, did it?' he says to the guy behind him.

Now obviously awake, he switches to the tactic of presenting an old reservation ticket taken from his wallet.

The guard smiles, clenches his teeth, draws back his cheeks and inhales while tilting his head to one side. This is Japanese body language for – surely you are not attempting to pretend that you don't understand that this reservation ticket is for another train, and then expect me to believe it.

The free cigarette-vending-machine man is watching this exchange with an expression of hope and concern. He has, through his gift, demonstrated his friendship towards the Englishman, and wants hard to believe that this Englishman won't make him feel a fool in so misplacing both his trust and his cigarettes.

Under pressure from the guard and the watching cigarette man, and perhaps from the gratefulness he feels towards the Sapporeans, the Englishman cracks. It is the worst attempted blag I have ever seen.

Three burly lads, whose mere presence would have been enough to turn away hardened teams of British railway guards, have been defeated by a small tubby Oriental who merely sucked in his cheeks. Because, once the first had cracked and paid the five hundred yen (three-pound) surcharge, the other two realise they are no match for this Eastern wizard and pay up too.

'Same?' asks the guard of them, ostensibly meaning the surcharge, but probably meaning: 'Are you as weak and cowardly as your big friend, girl-boy?'

'Yes, same please.'

But what makes this moment, and shows how quickly Japan can get to you, is the way the first lad responded to being rumbled. He was strapping, his skull all bone, muscle and skin, but he dropped his head and hunched his shoulders and, though he could never be unobtrusive, he made himself as small as he possibly could. It was an action that wasn't, but could in time become, something like an apologetic bow.

The shinkansen slows down as it approaches Sendai and moans like a woman in a particularly tragic Japanese drama. Then to add chagrin to humiliation, the three of them get off with me. If they could have held out a mere minute more they would have pulled it off. They would have become black-belt blaggers: the only English I ever saw in Japan to get away with sitting in a reserved compartment without a ticket. But they were just white belts really.

It's dark in Sendai and it's late, and I had made all sorts of diligent plans to find a cheap hotel. But when I go to the information booth and ask they tell me that every hotel is booked up.

'*What about a capsule hotel?*' I ask.

Capsule hotels are rows of bed-sized compartments with just enough room to lie down in. They are just like cryogenic sleeping pods in sci-fi films except that they don't include the 1,000-year cryogenic sleep facility, so when you wake up it is only the next morning.

'*Sometimes they don't like to have foreigners.*'

'*But I am Japanese speak foreigner.*'

'*As I say, but you can certainly try.*'

But I am glad to hear that all the hotels are full and that the capsule hotels won't take me. It means I have no option but to walk the 50 yards to the nearest luxury hotel and stay the night there. It will certainly have rooms because it is the sort of place where the staff, who all speak some English, punch the room fee into a calculator using at least five key strokes, turn it round and show it to you just to make sure you fully understand the vast sum of money they are going to take off you.

But I am not daunted. I agree the fee, and from my room can listen to the sound of Mexicans drumming on the station forecourt. In luxury hotel rooms in Japan it is sometimes difficult to see what luxury you are paying for. As I am only paying for the room, none of this luxury can have gone into the food, although it is possible to get a larger rate (six key stokes) that includes breakfast and an evening meal. But you should never do it, as a Japanese breakfast of fish, raw egg and rice is not something that is guaranteed to massage your early morning fragility back to mental wholeness. Nor can any of the luxury have gone into the size of the room. There is a capsule bathroom and a three-quarter bed that only leaves enough floor space to get inside them both. The con's do tend to be slightly more mod' than cheaper hotels: the air conditioning might have a dial rather than just high and low switches, but after a few seconds of playing with the dial it doesn't seem a significant bonus. No, all the luxury in a Japanese luxury hotel has gone into the foyer. Space being at such a premium in Japan, hotels like the Hotel Metropolitan in Sendai demonstrate their superiority by having foyers that are bigger than Sapporo stadium. It is often further to walk from the entrance to the front desk than it is from the nearest railway station. These foyers are floored and walled in marble, gilded in gold, and are furnished with Second Empire antiques. In order to maximise my investment in the hotel I spend as much time in the foyer as possible.

All Japanese hotels, luxury or otherwise, include two pay-per-view porn channels, which can be paid for either brazenly at the front desk when you check out, or discreetly with a card purchased from machines located near the lifts on every floor. There are usually three pay-per-view channels. The third shows bad American movies and acts simply as an alibi channel so that, if anyone sees you purchasing a card from the machine, you can hold your head up and pretend that you have a burning desire to see *Look Who's Talking Three*.

One of the oddest things about Japanese porn is the fact that they are not allowed to show pubic hair. Japanese pornographers get round this by pixiliating any pudenda that appear. Whenever the action gets intimate the problem area is covered with waves of large throbbing pixels, their size out of all proportion to any pixels you see in real life. Porn without pubes does seem pointless, and indeed there are always several longueurs when the screen becomes entirely filled with undulating blankness. The solution everyone finds independently is to screw up your eyes to near blindness and then at least you can see what is going on.

Whether you want to see what is going on is another matter. There are only two variants of Japanese porn: you can either watch porn actresses being degraded or real women being humiliated. The first variant involves too much S&M, simulated rape and bizarre mother-love fantasies for most trueborn Englishmen. But the real-women shows, despite the final ritualistic act of humiliation, do have some documentary interest. These involve one man with a hand-held, or a two- or three-man film crew, propositioning ordinary Japanese women in the street and asking if they would be interested in being filmed while they have sex (with all the film crew). Whether these women know they will end up on a Japanese hotel porn show is unclear (because my Japanese isn't up to it), but there is no doubt that they are volunteering.

Although this is quite fun at the beginning, towards the end the Japanese men making the film cannot help themselves. When each woman is being chatted up her individualism is apparent in her clothes, her hair, her make-up and her expressions. But as each film progresses she slowly loses everything that distinguishes her as an individual. Her clothes go first (obviously, this is porn); her hair and make-up become dishevelled; her expressions fix into a rictus grimace of pleasure-pain. Then for the *coup de grâce* the man withdraws and ejaculates over her breasts, the camera coming up to a man's standing height and looking down onto the naked, vulnerable, bespattered and slowly twisting any-woman that she has become.

Afterwards they may share a cigarette and a discussion.

'*I'm sorry I came too quickly,*' says the man politely.

'*Not at all,*' she replies kindly.

Except that the Japanese use 'go' rather than 'come' when they talk about orgasm. '*I'm sorry I went too quickly,*' was what he literally said. It would be tempting to see this as telling. At orgasm, the Japanese soul leaves its selfless, community-centred life to be for just a moment in a place of pure individual pleasure, while English-speaking souls are arriving at the ultimate point of self-fulfilment for the self-centred individualists that they are. But it's probably not true.

You have to pay for the porn, but the snuff movies come for free. On the commercial channels whole shows are devoted to replaying news clips and security-camera footage of people falling from buildings, being shot by robbers, sucked into jet engines, gored by bulls and set alight. In effect, it's a Japanese 'You've Been Flamed'. Occasionally, as in the porn movies, they will interview survivors just to show that they are all right. But they don't always do it, and the conclusion then must be that you have just been entertained by watching someone die.

KICKING

The next morning I go to the bus station to take a bus to the other end of town where I believe there will be a cheaper, tiny foyered hotel. I have now given up attempting to use my Japanese and use the tactic of just standing around looking lost. If you stand there they will come. And very quickly they do. Unfortunately the quantity of the help the Japanese give is in direct disproportion to its quality. Even after being helped by two members of the public and one of the bus station staff, I still end up on a bus that goes the wrong way round a huge circuit of the city. But I can't be bothered to get off and haul my bags back to the bus-stop so I spend 45 minutes on a journey that should have taken me five.

Japanese buses are as impressive as their trains and are designed like their books. You get on at the back, and get off at the front. You pay the driver on exiting and you don't need to tell him your starting point because as you get on you take a ticket with a number on it from a machine by the door. The price is shown next to your ticket number on an electronic board above the driver's head, the amount increasing the further from your starting point you travel.

This system, like many Japanese systems, relies entirely on honesty. Obviously if you take as long a journey as I was doing, and haven't been so foolish as to advertise your presence by being Caucasian, you could just nab a ticket when the bus reaches the stop before your destination and pay a much cheaper fare. But of course no one ever does. It's like revolving sushi restaurants where the colour of the plates indicates the price of the dish. At the end of your meal they calculate the bill by counting the plates you have left on the counter. For some reason, probably because we were brought up on heist films and individualism, Japan makes every Westerner feel like a criminal mastermind. While I can spot the loopholes in their systems, it never seems to occur to the Japanese to hide the plates, just as it never seems to occur to them to grab a cheaper ticket on the buses. In fact, Japan flatters you twice: first by convincing you that you are a criminal genius, and second by allowing you to demonstrate your moral strength by resisting the temptation to use your powers for evil.

So, having sat on the bus with all the time in the world to contemplate my Christ-like resistance to temptation, I finally get to a business hotel with a small foyer and am able to pay half the price for pretty much the same-sized room with the same facilities.

The first people I meet that morning when I eat breakfast in McDonald's are a chubby Swedish couple.

'Nothing is ever ready,' the woman sighs. She holds up two, then three fingers to illustrate how many minutes she has been asked to wait. 'I am on holiday so it doesn't matter, but if I wasn't on holiday . . .'

She breaks off to indicate that her wrath would be beyond words. She has a point though. The Japanese have made almost everything the West has given them quicker and more efficient: cars, videos, tape recorders, motorbikes, computer games. But as they couldn't do anything with fast food they decided to slow it down, just like they did with the making of a cup of tea.

'And it's difficult to get them to understand,' the Swedish woman adds. 'I get very unpatient.'

'Do you think that might be because you use words like unpatient?'

But I don't really say this, though I want to, because these are the first people I have met since Sapporo who are moaning about Japan. But of course they haven't had their Sapporo. Instead I ask if it might have anything to do with her accent.

'No,' she snaps, 'they just can't understand English.'

'You make it hard for us, eh?' chips in the man, referring to our immortal victory over the South American Hun.

'You make it hard for us, I think,' I say, just as their Big Macs appear and as a prelude to taking my leave. I am referring to the draw we played with them.

That night I go out on the streets to see how well the Mexicans party (they beat Ecuador that afternoon) and how the Japanese are doing in their game against Russia.

The streets are deserted, and it seems like England when a World Cup game is on except I have nothing to compare it to. It may just be Sendai on Sunday.

I find some Mexicans and a big group of Japanese gathered in a covered and pedestrianised shopping street in the centre of town. They are watching Japan's game against Russia on a television which has been set up in the window of a *pachinko* parlour: a place where tired Japanese go to play a skill-less bagatelle-like game which features ball-bearings passing at random in front of the player's eyes. There are about 200 people here, the majority of them sitting on the pavement, with a circle of people standing around them. Most are Japanese and there are only about 20 or so Mexicans, all of whom seem to be wearing floppy sombreros.

I have seen Swedes in Viking horns, Irish dressed as leprechauns, English wearing crowns and Japanese in samurai hairpieces, but the sombrero must be the perfect item of clothing for donning to demonstrate your ethnicity. A fan's football shirt advertises his or her nationality, but many supporters seem to feel that they need something more, some additional piece of kit to show your cultural orientation to the passport-fact of your nationality. The sombrero is easily put on and taken off, and it says hot and unhurried – for who can hurry with a sombrero on? – flamboyant and unreserved. It is as big a statement as a woman's wedding hat in England, and the impact is not reduced even if everyone else is wearing them.

The Japanese have not yet found that essential piece of additional kit, and they may never do, because they seem to like the group uniformity that the ubiquitous blue shirts give them. It is noticeable that, for all the named replica shirts, the Nakatas and Inamotos, the most popular shirt is the one without a name. It is also noticeable that every Japanese supporter is under the age of 25. Unlike the English with their hoolidads, neither here nor anywhere in Japan did I ever see a shirt-wearing supporter over a quarter of a century old.

The telly is so small that apart from the people at the front of the crowd no one can really see what is going on. From where I am standing at the back I can hardly see which side has the ball and which way they are heading. The crowd helps though. They groan when Russia has the ball and cheer when the Japanese advance.

At half-time the Mexicans lead the Japanese in a Mexican wave. One of the Mexicans tries to tempt a solitary Croatian to get up and dance. There are drinking competitions. One lad, naked from the waist up and with the characters for Japan painted onto his back, has whisky poured down his throat by a friend from the height of about a foot. He has a loudhailer and appears to have put himself in charge. He leads the seated spectators in a few chants of 'Nippon'.

In the second half Japan score but the crowd is desperate for them to get another goal. They have plenty of chances but fail with them all, while the Russians continue to counterattack. Japan has never won a World Cup game so everyone understands how momentous this would be if they hold on. A big bullish lad towards the front of the seated crowd tries to lead them off with the mournful notes of the national anthem, but no one joins him. There was the same reluctance on the subway in Sapporo. The 120-year-old Japanese national anthem, 'Kimigayo', which expresses the hope that the Emperor will live for 8,000 generations, was only made the official national anthem just after the World Cup. It is associated with right-wing ultra-nationalism and its adoption by the state caused protests in the Japanese parliament. It was as if someone has seriously suggested adding the controversial 'No surrender' lyric to 'God Save the Queen'. Many young Japanese people will not sing 'Kimigayo', and at graduation ceremonies in high schools whole classes will refuse to participate.

When the whistle blows there is a second or two of vast relief, and then a sudden surge of celebration. They leap to their feet and dance and chant 'Nippon, Nippon' and hug each other. The lone Croatian is thrown into the air. One young man lies at my feet in emotional exhaustion shaking his head and smiling up at me. Another climbs the streetlight and balances on top waving a Mexican flag. The failed instigator of 'Kimigayo' shouts at him and, in an identical moment to the one in Sapporo, tries to pull the foreign flag out of his hand. But the lad on the light is too quick. Seeing someone else occupying pole position is too much for the man with the naked torso and he too clambers up the lamppost.

'*It's dangerous, dangerous,*' shouts the lad already up there.

Torso, whom we have already seen drink half a bottle of whisky, isn't to be reasoned with and the other lad gives up his place to him and climbs down. Someone hands Torso his loudhailer and he begins to chant at the crowd. But they don't seem to want him as a focus, though they want something. They gather in groups around other individuals and jump up and down shouting 'Nippon'.

Ten yards away somebody starts to let off firecrackers and fireworks. Given that this is a covered shopping mall this isn't a brilliant idea. The fireworks shoot up, smash against the transparent cover and shower sparks and phosphorescent globules onto the crowd below. Two security guards walk past, but they can do nothing. One of them is on the phone.

Everything about this moment says something about the contemporary Japanese. They have come to the centre of town because they want to share the moment with their peers, but they have been unable to find anywhere other than in front of a tiny telly in a shop window. There aren't enough bars or open-air venues showing the match (though there are ticketed indoor events). The bars and restaurants, run by older people, have not anticipated the demand. And there is something odd about their celebrations. It is as if they do not know what to do. This is the first time they have had to celebrate a World Cup victory, and there is only so long that you can jump up and down chanting 'Nippon'. They won't sing 'Kimigayo', but they have as yet no other songs to sing. There are the fireworks and the one or two people climbing the streetlights, but the rest of them are waiting for something. They just do not know what it is.

It is like watching history. Partly it is their obvious youth and the lack of any tradition, partly it is all the sitting crossed-legged in the street and the all-you-need-is-love belief that if they want it hard enough anything can happen, but what it reminds me of is the 1960s. Here is a generation exploring a new form of behaviour, participating in something that their baseball- and sumo-following parents and grandparents cannot understand.

Then something extraordinary happens. Initially it is only a few policemen at the end of the street, but the first thing they do is block it off and park a water cannon on the intersection. They let people leave but won't let anybody come in to fuel the crowd. Then another group begins to work its way slowly down the street.

'What's going on,' I ask, 'why are they doing this?'

'Look, they are just forming a line down the street to keep the way open,' says an American next to me. 'Don't ever ask why the Japanese do things, they always have a reason.'

But it isn't Sapporo. They aren't just keeping the road open, and the definiteness of the American's reply conceals his own puzzlement. The police are cautiously making the chanting crowd aware of their presence. One policeman films them with a video camera while plain-clothes photographers take less obtrusive shots. They get the response they want. The crowd begins to disperse from its edges inwards. It isn't heavy-handed, they are not looking for a confrontation, but they are not going to let this spontaneous gathering continue.

There is an Englishman beside me now. His name is Neil and he is a security consultant from Hong Kong so has technical expertise.

'See the guys in the suits with the earpieces and walkie-talkies?' he says. 'They're in charge.'

The uniformed policemen are young, and there are others in black rain jackets who look tougher and more experienced, but Neil is right, the portly middle-aged men in cheap suits are the ones in charge.

'I can understand them filming us,' I say. 'But I don't understand why they are filming their own people.'

'It's for court purposes,' Neil says. 'If someone claims something happened they can show it to the court. It's for their own protection.

'It's very clever what they did with us,' he says generally of the Japanese organisation. 'All the liaison with the fans is done by pretty girls in polo-necks who are never going to be the focus of any trouble. The police just stay in the background. But here they're just doing what they're trained for, they have spent years preparing for this.'

But it was difficult to believe that these young people were a threat to anyone. Just the presence of the police would have stopped the fireworks and brought down the one or two who climbed the streetlights. But the police wanted more than this. They wanted complete order. In Sapporo they had shown that they would tolerate our singing, dancing and drinking on the street, but here they were not prepared to tolerate exactly the same behaviour from their own citizens. Perhaps they were aware that gentle pressure wouldn't work on the English, but that it would work on their own young people.

Neil and I watch as the crowd evaporates, except it isn't evaporation, it is the cooler elements being stripped away while just the hotheads remain. Occasionally the crowd will recoalesce around some Mexicans who try to keep the party going, but there aren't enough gaijin to provide an armature for the Japanese. Within half an hour there are only a few dozen Japanese supporters left.

We have been forced all the way down the street by the pressure from the police and we think the night is over, but when we get to the far end one of the Mexicans takes a football and begins to juggle it.

He starts by balancing the ball on his head and on his foot to applause, then bounces it off his shoulder and knees. Then he begins to head it, his neck bent back and his body arched and his eyes to heaven as if he were experiencing the divine. Slowly, and with the ball still bouncing on his forehead, he begins to take his shirt off until it is bunched around his neck. Then in one swift movement while the ball is in the air he takes it over his head. The two dozen of us watching this start to cheer. Then he reverses the process and puts it back on. Next he balances the ball on the back of his neck and drops slowly towards the floor, and still with the ball behind his head, he does press-ups on the ground before returning to a standing position. He keeps the ball in the air for 15 minutes.

'Look at him,' says Neil, '40-something and with a paunch and just look at his skill. What English player could do that?'

This was how the World Cup was supposed to be: Europeans, Asians and South Americans enjoying the party, mixing together, showing each other their party tricks, having fun. But not the Japanese. They are only allowed to watch.

Eventually even the far end of the street empties of people and I go back towards my cheaper hotel. Around the corner five buses full of riot police are moving into position.

In Sendai the police stopped them, but on the television news that night they show what happened in other cities when the Japanese supporters found their focus. In Osaka they jumped off bridges into the canals, and in another of Tokyo's nightlife areas, Shinjuku, two telephone boxes were smashed up. The newscaster was stunned by this. '*Homu sappota*,' he kept saying, and he would give the word a different intonation each time. Sometimes it sounded like a question, sometimes like a lament, sometimes it was said authoritatively to make sure that his viewers fully understood that it was not foreigners but home supporters who had done this.

Next morning, as I have breakfast in a bakery coffee shop, I talk to an old man with cancer flecks on his skin. He is off to play the board game Go with other old men, as he does every week. 'No gambling, no drinking, no smoking,' he says, either of the rules of the club or of the rules of his own life. He likes baseball and sumo, but his three grandchildren all belong to soccer teams.

Go is very simple and very hard. The game is played with black and white counters on a board made up of a grid with hundreds of intersections. The players take turns and try to cordon off as much space on the board with their counters as they can. The importance of any individual counter is dependent on its relationship with all the others, and commentators on Japan have been tempted to use the game as a metaphor for Japanese culture. Particularly when Go is compared to the West's most demanding board game: chess.

In chess there is a class division between the rulers and their pawns. The undistinguishable pawns have very little freedom of movement and can only progress forward through the lifetime of the game. Only rarely does one of them ever live long enough to become one of the rulers: a queen, a knight, a bishop or a rook. No pawn can ever become king. The rulers, however, have distinct personalities and powers, so much so that the capture of one of them is the entire point of the game. In Go, space is power, and Japan is indeed a cramped country which is grid-lined with rice paddies. In chess, the individual is king.

The difference between Go and chess may seem as slipperily insignificant as the difference between 'go' and 'come'. But it is impossible not to believe that the games people enjoy are as characteristic of their culture as the books they read or the films they watch. The old man likes the monocultural sport of sumo and the baseball he learned from the Americans after the war. But his grandchildren prefer a game that is neither nationalist nor pro-American in its orientation. They prefer to show their patriotism in the global game.

There is a commotion at the counter. A group of six gaijin is getting coffee and cakes.

'Mexicans,' says the old man with a gentle sniff as he leaves, 'I don't think they understand traffic signals.'

Nor do they understand the correct procedure for buying coffee and cakes from a café bakery.

The correct procedure is to choose the patisserie you want with the tongs provided and put it on plastic tray. You then go to the counter and say 'eat in' or 'take away' and order your beverage. If you are a gaijin the assistant will usually confirm by pointing towards the tables or out of the door. You then are told and/or shown the price. There is a small plastic tray for you to put your money on, so avoiding any of the messy touching of hands and scrabbling for coins that we do in England. It is very important to say or do nothing more than this.

For gaijin there is one further rule. It is best never to choose a patisserie which may have a filling. Doughnuts, rolls and buns may contain something that could ruin your morning: a bean-paste centre, a bitter plum with a stone in it, or curry paste. Even if you can read Japanese it is still best to avoid the possibility. Of course you could ask, but as soon as you get to the level of Japanese which allows you to say, 'Is there anything in this delicacy that will make me sick?' you tend not to say it, as you realise how offensive it would be. Learning Japanese is like this. All you are doing is learning not to say the things you thought you were learning Japanese to say. The best items to buy in Japanese bakeries are flat things like Danish pastries or pizza breads – where you can see what has been added to them.

Perhaps this is what has happened with the Mexicans, a queue of patient, but slightly tense Japanese forming behind them, one of them must have realised that the tempting doughnut is a stodgy stooge containing bean-paste.

Service in Japan is commonly regarded as the best in the world. Unfortunately the Japanese love of ornamental communication means that most of the service is very ritualistic and relies on the customer knowing exactly what to do and saying nothing. In the lower-level service jobs, the bank clerk, shop assistant, waiter or waitress has a formulaic series of movements and words to express his or her gratitude to the customer for patronising his or her business, and doesn't expect to be interrupted by any contribution from the customer. Even saying thank you can cause a problem. Coming from England I have never been able to master this, and use the most honorific thank you I know to express my pleasure at being allowed to spend my own money. This or any other unscripted comment or action can often spook the young men and women behind the counter into a go-slow and then a standstill.

This is what is happening to the Mexicans. They are going backwards and forwards to the shelves of cakes adding to their orders in lively Latin fashion and the girls behind the counter have been stunned into immobility.

Eventually, however, this commotion settles down and the Mexicans come and sit near me. They have come to a café bakery for breakfast for the same reason as me: they have discovered that breakfast is the one meal of the day when you don't want to experiment with Japanese food. I ask them if they mind telling me what they think of Japan.

The first thing they tell me is that they are Ecuadorians. I have no idea where Ecuador is other than South America and know nothing else about their country.

There are six of them, two women and four men. The two women and two of the men are from the US and obviously speak perfect English, the other two speak mainly Spanish.

'Japan is beautiful,' they all agree, 'and everyone is so nice.'

'Sometimes they are too nice though,' muses one of the women, all of us gaijin having been shocked by the crazed kamikaze kindness of our hosts.

'The only trouble is finding somewhere to watch the match,' says one of the men. 'It gives the impression they are not into it. Even in the bars, we had to ask them to get a television out for us and they didn't like it. The event's fairly colourful for the Japanese, but not for us.'

'Has it changed your view of the Japanese?' I ask.

'It has confirmed it more than anything, about how polite and punctual they are. Four of us are from the US so we see a lot of Japanese, but in Ecuador you only see them going mountain climbing or to the Galapagos Islands.'

I am grateful that they have given me a clue about where Ecuador is. Images of Darwin's voyage on *The Finch* to study the various species on the islands come to mind.

'To see the famous beagles?' I almost ask.

'You see their money, their cameras, their moving mechanically from place to place. But here they are more relaxed and they go mad for the salsa. But I have seen the Japanese over-react. They closed off an entire square in order to arrest one Englishman. But we're the ones who benefit. We're the ones who feel safe.

'The other fans have been great though,' he adds quickly. 'And the English have been very friendly. We have common ground with them. We love football and we love beer and we know how to party. They don't ask where Ecuador is which has surprised me, and some of them know things about our football leagues.'

I am glad I chose not to ask them where Ecuador is and I too am impressed by the English fans' knowledge of their football.

'But trying to get the results has been hell. They don't seem to show the highlights on television. We had to buy a Japanese newspaper and try to work out the results of the US game from that.'

'So what happens now you've lost?'

'Mexico has to beat Italy and we have to win by three goals to get through.' He shrugs, 'A lot of stars have to be aligned for that to happen.'

They sounded just like we did a few days ago. But they hadn't had their Sapporo.

The next day I go over to the coast near Saitama to see Matsushima or Poets' Islands, officially one of the three most beautiful sights in Japan. The Japanese love ranking and will grade almost anything. With the widespread popularity of the Japanese martial arts, probably the whole of the Western world knows that the different-coloured belts indicate different levels of skill. A good proportion of people may also know that the black belt only indicates basic competence and that after a black belt you can go up another ten levels (or *dan*). Some may even know that the coloured belts are just for kids. But this isn't peculiar to the martial arts, it's applied to everything. You can get a figurative black belt in Go and even, I think, in flower arranging. So Poets' Islands must have fought it out with other beautiful sights in a nasty scrap of comparative sunsets to get into the top three.

Poets' Islands are undeniably pretty, but as poets, including Basho, ran out of things to say about them 500 years ago, there is no point in my describing them. All I can say is that some of the islands are connected to the shore by bridges that would fail Western health and safety standards as well as those for access for people with disabilities.

The bridges are painted in fire-extinguisher red, and Western visitors might be fooled into thinking that this indicates that they are emergency exits for use in some island-studded bay catastrophe such as a tsunami. They are not. The bridges are made of two lines of planks a foot-fall apart over joists that are a thigh's width apart, and you cannot move over them very quickly because of the holes. One of the techniques used in Japanese garden design is to control the speed that the visitor moves through the landscape. The placing of stepping-stones will be dependent on the type of progress the gardener wants to encourage: far apart for leaping; close together for slow. The bridges had the same effect. You had to look down to stop stepping through the holes and so saw the sea slopping away beneath your feet, and you could only look at the view when you stopped.

Obviously these bridges were designed only for the able-bodied, and while I was there two middle-aged women helped their elderly mother over one of them. It took an age, and, if he had seen it happening, the designer of the bridges would have been as angry as a film director with a projector that was running slow.

Aesthetics had triumphed over access, but in Japan everything triumphs over access. You can see this in the Japanese attitude to physical disability. While there are lines of yellow studded tiles along pavements to help the blind, it is very rare you see anything that might be of help to people with physical disabilities. On the trains there are icons above the priority seats to show who they are for: parents with young children, pregnant women; old people with sticks and people with casts on their legs; all the temporal infirmities that might befall an able-bodied human being. But there is no indication that there is anybody who might have permanent difficulties with access.

So that was Matsushima. If Basho had been stumped so would I be.

The next day England are due to play Nigeria in Osaka, so early the next morning I take a shinkansen down to Tokyo then change to one for Osaka.

England has nothing comparable to Osaka. Technically it is Japan's second city, but technically Birmingham is England's second city and all non-Brummie English know how misleading this is. Historically Osaka is more like its first. The city lies to the south-west of Tokyo in the west country close to the country's ancient capital Nara and the city that was its capital for 1,000 years, Kyoto. It is almost as if somewhere near a Winchester that had remained the seat of the English kings until the nineteenth century, there had grown up a port city which partook of the ancient monarchical and religious links of the West Country and which looked down on London as a parvenu. If there is any candidate it is Bristol, but it would have to be a Bristol with the population of Birmingham and the panache of Manchester.

Between Tokyo and Osaka there is a mountain that has an iconic and spiritual significance for the Japanese. Between London and Bristol there is a mountain which has an iconic and spiritual significance for a small number of the English. In any Japanese-style ranking of the most iconic mountains in the world Mount Fuji would probably outclass Glastonbury Tor both because of its actual size and its relative weight in the minds of the people who live in the countries which surround them. But it's in the right area.

At Tokyo station the English are gathering. They are being sucked out of the city and funnelled into shinkansen down to Osaka.

The lad I chat to on the train is going home after the match. He is from Carlisle and he has come to stand with me in the connecting corridor next to the smoking carriage. He has a seat in there but does not smoke and the grey air was getting to him, so he is standing by the door of the shinkansen in the place where on English trains you can stand by the open window. But the relief is psychological and nostalgic, for the shinkansen windows do not open.

'I'm missing pies the most,' he says. 'But tomorrow night I'll be having pie and chips in front of *Corrie*.'

Up in Sapporo he had been interviewed by a Japanese news crew and asked what he thought about the trouble.

'What trouble?' he had asked.

'The smashing of a sports goods shop window and the stealing of some shirts.'

He had laughed then and he was laughing now at the disproportionality of his expectations and theirs.

'"That's not trouble," I said. There's more trouble on a Saturday night in Carlisle.'

He has his own tale of kamikaze kindness. We all do: the sleepy Swiss with his invitation to spend the night at the foreman's house; the failed blagger on the train to Sendai and his encounter with cigarette-vending-machine man; Neil, the security consultant, who had told me that in Sapporo a salaryman had rushed out of a hostess bar to donate an almost full bottle of whisky to the party which 'must have cost him over a hundred pounds'.

'We went to the beer hall in Sapporo,' says the lad from Carlisle, 'and as we were coming out my mate realised he had dropped his wallet with everything in it, his rail pass as well.'

Next to the match tickets, the rail pass is the most valuable thing we have as it gets us free onto nearly all JR trains.

'We told the girls behind the counter, and they were really concerned and started going through the rubbish for us. Can you imagine that happening in England? It would just be a shrug and a "It's your problem, mate."'

Absent-mindedly I light a cigarette, but remembering his reason for being here I stub it out in the ashtray.

'Don't be stupid,' he says. 'Go on, smoke, don't worry about me. We retraced our steps, you always do that but it never works, but this time it did. As we were coming out he had got his camera out and it must have fallen out there because it was still there. So we went back and really apologised to the girls.

'They went through the rubbish for us,' he says again, unconsciously polishing the anecdote he may tell for the rest of his life.

English from other carriages who want to smoke come up and join us, and soon the air around the Carlisle man is greyer than the smoking carriage. But he doesn't seem to mind. He is listening to the others tell their own tales: a Singaporean ex-pat who at the airport had left his baby's pillow on the bus between the terminal and the aircraft, 'I thought "I'll never see that again", but they told me to wait and in half an hour they brought it back to me.' Everything we say is about how wonderful the Japanese are.

But the longer you stay in Japan, the more this kindness and courtesy fades to become like the background noise of the shop assistants' thank-yous. The memories you treasure are the ones that confirm your faith in human nature, what you never forget is being treated badly. These occasions are so rare that they stand out as revealingly as acts of selfless generosity do in England.

I will never forget the woman in one of the station kiosks who tried to rip me off. I had bought some fags and some Coke and gave the woman a ten thousand yen note. She returned the change for a thousand. This is the monetary equivalent of giving somebody fifty quid and getting change for a fiver in return. Bless her, she tried to short-change me. I paused for a moment. 'Ay ay ay ay,' she said when she saw I hadn't walked off and realised I must understand Japanese money. Quickly she gave me the other nine thousand yen. It was so unusual and so generous of her to provide me with that moment I will never forget that I nearly asked if I could take her photograph.

Further down the train to Osaka there is a scene of very English chaos and debauchery.

The door to the carriage has been jammed open and an Arsenal fan is trying to tie his flag, the Arsenal cannon, across the entrance.

'I have got to get the cannon in,' he says to no one.

Inside it is chaos or as close to chaos as it ever gets on a Japanese train. Something alcoholic has been spilled on the floor and two uniformed Japanese guards are on their knees trying to mop it up with wodges of paper. In front of them, a small drunk Englishman is standing in the middle of the carriage shouting at some English girls. 'Shut it! Shut it!' he shouts. His voice is aiming for a parody of anger but his pointing and thrusting of his torso is less of a parody. Nobody ever need stagger on a shinkansen, they are too smooth, but he is staggering from side to side in the aisle. His brain can just keep his voice functioning but can no longer keep his body under control. The girls are laughing at him. Surreally, into this chaos comes a Japanese woman and her 12-year-old son. Would it be possible to have a photo?

Calmly and happily she goes to stand just in front of the drunk and gets her son to take a photograph. Behind her, the drunk, his face transformed into a Benny Hill leer, rubs his hands then puts them close to her buttocks, clenching and unclenching his fingers. The son, who must be able to see this through his viewfinder, understandably fluffs the shot a couple of times but finally takes one: a tableau of a happy Japanese mother, a leering drunk and two guards cleaning up after the English.

What this photograph will illustrate is how safe the Japanese feel in their own country. On an English train everybody who was not involved would be trying not to get involved. But the Japanese mother treats the presence of a drunk Englishman like a circus act into which she can insert herself without danger, as if the drunk is a character in a Bacchanalian Disney World. The other Japanese passengers in the same carriage have the same reaction. They are curious, watchful, and mildly discomforted by the possibility that they might, through no actions of their own, become that most awful of all things for a Japanese: involuntarily obtrusive. But they are not nervous, and consequently there isn't any of the tension that is experienced in England when someone behaves drunkenly and loutishly. It is a nervousness that creates tension and so exacerbates the situation, and this is something that never happened in Japan. Their confidence prevented it.

I meet Rob and his mate at the station and we take a short taxi ride to our hotel. Or it should be a short taxi ride. Unless you are going to one of the big foyered hotels, Japanese taxi drivers, for all their white-gloved ungeezerly service, never know exactly where they are going. Understanding this, back-street hotels like the one we are booked into provide their customers with small address cards with a map on them, and Rob has been sent one of these. Unfortunately the maps don't help because they are so large scale they will only get you to within a few hundred yards of the hotel, and once off the main road you inevitably get lost in the warren of streets and alleys. Most of the fare in a Japanese taxi is taken up by these last few hundred yards. You are then at the mercy of the taxi driver and his mobile phone. What follows is just as formulaic as a shop assistant's gestures. The taxi driver will make a couple of attempts to pretend that he knows where he is going, and then ask to reconsult the map. Having done this he will scratch his head as if this is the first time that he has ever been unable to find what he is looking for. He will then make another couple of turns. He then gets out a mobile phone and rings his office. Two more turns and now even he is lost in relation to the main road and he does the sensible thing and rings the hotel on his mobile phone. At this point, in what looks like a gesture of kindness, and which probably is in his mind a gesture of kindness, he switches off the meter. He then has to refind the main road and sometimes even be talked in by the hotel receptionist. The hotel map-makers probably provide their services free to the hotels and are probably employed by the taxi firms.

We dump our bags and walk back to the station to get a train to the stadium where we meet Ken and Gemma. Everything about Osaka is different from the other two games. The stadium is in the centre of a built-up area and there is none of the airport grandeur of Saitama or the futurism of Sapporo. You come out of the station, cross a dual carriageway and into a small park where there are too many people for the space. The initial ticket check is less rigorous and the funnels of crowd barriers behind it are easily leapt. The police also have a nonchalance about them that I haven't seen before. Rob says they are used to riots in Osaka, and the police certainly give the impression that the arrival of the English is not the biggest thing that has ever happened to them. Every policeman in Tokyo and Sapporo, as professional as they were, looked nervous, as if he might be called upon to do something that he had never done before. But the Osakan police loll around looking unimpressed. The England crowd, too, is less excited. Obviously Nigeria have none of the credibility of the Argentines, and we know that with a win and a draw already achieved, a lot of stars would have to be misaligned for us to fail to go through to the second round. The team seems to share the mood because the

KICKING

fixture is played as if it were a dull necessity, an engagement that has to be got through in order to progress to the next round.

'Come on, play like Sapporo,' people shout with irritation in the hot sunlight. 'We want to finish top.'

But it seems the management does not want us to finish top of the group. If we come top we have to go down to Oita. It is hot in Osaka but it will be far hotter in the far south, where we would play Senegal under the afternoon sun. If we come second, we go to northern Niigata and play Denmark in the cool evening. 'And those Africans can get nasty when they get desperate,' says someone trying to account for the lacklustre play. But the crowd is desperate for certainty and as the game bores on they become more demanding and more critical.

It is not like the Japanese who will their team to victory, every touch applauded, every opposition attack dreaded. There is a more critical, more cynical realisation that we could lose, and lose everything. Our irritation is in proportion to our impotence, and there is a dark mood gathering of thwarted desire. For how would we reconcile our pride if, having taunted the French and the Argentine, we fail to go through?

Somehow news comes through from the other game that Sweden are drawing with Argentina 1–1. 'Rumour, Rumour,' repeats a cynical aggressive voice behind me, holding his negativity close. In the end it turns out to be true and we go through second in the group, but there is no pride in our performance.

The England team has made our travel plans for us, and back in Osaka's downtown Dotomburi we go through the guidebooks. Rob rings from a phone box on the street, but none of the hotels in Niigata have any vacancies, or say they don't.

'They will have been booked up by the Swedish,' Ken reasons, 'but the cancelled reservations might take a day or two to come through.'

'That's if they bother to cancel them,' says Rob. 'I mean I would, but . . .'

But perhaps the Swedish, like the two fast-food complainers, haven't been got by Japan.

So we leave the phone box. Rob goes into the middle of the road to pee against one of the trees in the central reservation. But on seeing the police who are already massing across the road he decides against it.

'It's not illegal,' he says, 'but they might just decide to hassle me.'

I think as a matter of law that this is technically inaccurate, but you do often seen Japanese men peeing in the streets. And it would be unfair to penalise anyone for it because many of the men's toilets often only have one door so the urinals can be seen. In some stations the women's toilets are actually through the men's. Also, Japanese female cleaners don't block off the doorway when they are cleaning the men's toilets and you just get into the habit of being Japanese and peeing while the woman is cleaning the urinal next to you. It's a habit that you only keep when you return to the UK for a short while.

So Rob nips down an alleyway only to meet a Japanese woman who calls him dirty.

'It's only because I'm a foreigner,' he complains. 'If it was a Japanese bloke she wouldn't think twice about it.'

While we are waiting for him I ask Gemma how it is she can reconcile being a left-wing internationalist (she used to work for the EU) and someone who is prepared to chant, 'You dirty Argie bastards'.

'You do take on a different persona when you go to a football match,' she says. 'I talk like that dun I, darling?'

She says that it isn't real, football, that certain things are allowable that wouldn't be in the real world but that the one thing she won't join in with or indeed tolerate is racism, which she differentiates from nationalism. And, on the train in Sapporo she had stood up for a young Japanese girl who was having her hair stroked by an English man in a way that was to Gemma and the others watching intolerable. This wasn't quite racism but it was exploitation and she uses it to illustrate her point.

Ken too is beginning to cotton on to the Japanese, but he is also versed in the ways of multiculturalism and he is unwilling to be definite because assuming people share characteristics because of their skin colour borders uncomfortably close to racism.

'I don't want to be patronising,' he says, 'but the Japanese act much more like foreigners when the foreigners are around.'

A low-slung American *Starsky and Hutch*-style car passes as we wait for him and the driver casually lifts his fist up to me in a nonchalant greeting. I just smile for a moment assuming he is going to say Beckham. He looks confused. Obviously he meant it as a challenge, but he had no finger gesture available to him to elaborate its meaning. I have never seen any fuck-you finger signs in Japan. Or of course he may have no fingers.

I am only in this city for 24 hours but there is also a nonchalance and a sophistication to its people that is very different from Tokyo. The women are cooler, less obviously impressed by the presence of large numbers of foreign men, and there isn't the drained look of the Tokyo salarymen and the desperate trendiness of the Tokyo girls. The faces that pass you on the street are full of character, and do not seem to fade into type.

We go to a restaurant and they go on to karaoke, but I go on alone to the Pig and Whistle, an English pub in the centre of Dotomburi. The pub is on the first floor, but is so packed that the English have taken over the Piaz Café below it simply because of its vertical proximity. There are English in the window above waving and chanting and more on the veranda of the café singing and chanting.

Osaka's police hang around outside. They don't bother to pretend that they are there to keep the roads open, and their riot buses are not hidden but drawn up on the streets opposite. They are doing nothing other than waiting for trouble.

An England fan is standing on a wall watching and talking to a policeman.

'Your country conquered Argentina,' says the policeman, 'like Falklands. Tell me the relationship between your country and Argentina.'

'It's friendly really,' says the fan, but he realises he cannot explain in basic English any more than the policeman has already grasped and gives up any attempt at further complexity. 'But we don't like Germany.'

I go up the stairs and queue outside the Pig and Whistle. A notice on the door says that they have been asked by the authorities to keep to the numbers prescribed so they are letting one in one out. It is about a 20-minute wait and the guy behind me tells a story about his father and the '66 World Cup. It is prompted because I tell him I only have tickets through to the quarter-finals and that I will then be begging.

'You never know,' he says. 'My father went to all England's games during the World Cup. He had a ticket for the final but he couldn't go. There was this kid who he had seen standing outside the other games, so when he saw him after the semi-final asking for a ticket he gave him his for free.'

'I'm not a cute kid.'

'You never know.'

Inside the pub there are shouts of 'We are English scum, we are English scum.'

Someone comes out. 'We're all going to the bridge in five minutes,' he says. I presume he means the same bridge the Japanese youths had jumped off after Japan beat Russia. But I want to keep my place in the queue, and ten minutes later nobody has left.

Inside the Pig and Whistle it is packed and sweaty and full of English flavour. As I make my way to the bar, the crowd starts to sing lustily: 'Rule Britannia', 'God Save the Queen', 'I am an Antichrist', 'Vindaloo' and 'Football's Coming Home': patriotism, monarchism, anarchism, and the paeans to curry and football. After these characteristic anthems of Englishness, about a fifth of the people there sing 'No Surrender'. Then, and only from a corner, from the people at the window who were waving, comes a low guttural chant of 'UDA, UDA'.

When I get to the bar I hear a voice I recognise.

'They're brilliant,' the voice says, 'I'm so proud of them.'

He is talking about the England crowd generally, and not the UDA boys.

'So it's back to Niigata again, back to fucking Niigata,' he adds.

NIIGATA PART ONE

Ireland 1 Cameroon 1
29 May–1 June

THE TRAIN CAME OUT OF THE TUNNEL AND INTO THE SLOW country.

Fucking Niigata, we had both been there before. On 1 June the town had hosted the opening game of Japan's World Cup, Ireland v. Cameroon, and we had both come up to this small provincial city for the game. He was a tout on the black market make, and I had come because it was the place I had lived in ten years before.

We had met on the station forecourt two days before the Ireland game, before England v. Sweden, before Sapporo, before even the humiliation of France in the opening game in South Korea. There were barrels of close-to-gaping tulips along all the pavements and a banner greeting the fans that hung in the overcast sky. But there was no one on the forecourt to welcome Irish fans to Niigata and Japan other than the English tout and his partner.

The fans had come on the shinkansen, through the tunnels of the Japanese mountains, through the canyons of Tokyo on subway trains, through the air itself in a long three-legged Celtic journey via Dublin, London and Frankfurt airports, only for the first people they met to be two English ticket touts.

Then a camera crew turned up, and it gave me hope that at least the local television station had realised that the arrival of the first World Cup fans needed to be marked with more than tulip barrels and welcome banners. The reporter spoke English so he could encourage the Irish to sing and holler, to olé Ireland, unfurl their flags and put on their silly hats.

KICKING

95

'What made you decide to come today?' I asked him.

'The opening game is in Korea,' he said, 'but this is the Japanese opening game so we thought we should cover it.'

'So where are you from?'

'Korea.'

He had the big round eyes liked by lenses the world over, even in Japan, so I hadn't spotted that he wasn't Japanese.

Eventually a local television crew did turn up, but only in the late afternoon when much of the excitement of the day had gone, and they hadn't bothered to send anyone who spoke English.

The only Japanese welcome for the Irish was one they had to find themselves: a small, temporary World Cup booth set up just outside the station. It was staffed by people who, from their willingness to help, were obviously volunteers, but who couldn't help me with what I wanted to know. When I asked if there was anywhere I could watch the opening ceremony and the France v. Senegal game from South Korea they were unsure. There was a conference, they didn't like to say no, but eventually they had to.

'Maybe you should go to a television shop,' suggested one.

On the other side of the great pavement U that is the station forecourt, buses circling the taxis queuing in its centre, there was a tourist office. It was staffed by a woman of a certain age, and from her I learned that there was at least an official indoor ticketed venue in which I could watch the Ireland game. But she spoke no English, this woman of a certain age, and she had to make two phone calls to find out about the TV venue. She never thought to direct me to the football booth across the way.

So, I wondered, if two English ticket touts and a Korean television crew could work out that there would be Irish fans around two days before the game, why couldn't Japanese television, and why wasn't there someone in the tourist booth who could speak English?

But it wasn't just organisations that seemed either uninterested or unprepared. Few of the thousands of Niigatans who passed through the station that day stopped to watch what must have been the strangest group of live foreigners they had ever seen. It was entertainment: the Irish, in their willingness to have an impromptu sing-song, were entertaining. These carnival moments were a spectacle, but there were no spectators. The Japanese walked past it as

Leprechauns being interviewed in Niigata
before Ireland's first match.

Police defending the integrity of the
pavement outside Niigata station.

Irish fans in the rain outside The Black Pig in Niigata.

English and Japanese partying in Odori Park, Sapporo,
before England v. Argentina.

A salaryman watches English fans in bemusement (Odori Park, Sapporo).

An appropriately clad Japanese girl makes the two-fingered gesture meaning peace (Odori park, Sapporo).

Cultural exchange (Odori Park, Sapporo).

A street cleaner retrieves his hat from
England fans (Odori Park, Sapporo).

A single Argentine fan with a message of peace, protected
by a Japanese steward (Sapporo Stadium).

England fans inside a bar greeting Japanese youths
after England beat Argentina (Sapporo).

A Japanese youth after encountering England fans
brandishing pens (Sapporo).

An exuberant England fan heads a restaurant lantern (Sapporo).

An England fan takes refreshment during the all-night party.

The difficulty of finding anywhere to watch the games illustrated in Niigata before England play Denmark.

After Japan go out, a policeman confronts an over-exuberant Japanese fan before arresting him.

The author (top) with his teaching colleagues before a party (1989).

if it was some strange altercation that had nothing to do with them, and, despite their reputation for inscrutability, you could actually see what they were thinking as they came towards the station.

'What's this? What is happening? Why are there so many crazed foreigners? Oh yes, of course, it must be the World Cup. How stupid of me to forget and not take steps to avoid it. Perhaps I should get out of here quickly before they either kill or embarrass me, or both.'

So, apart from English entrepreneurship, two days before the game the national characteristics on display in this provincial city were Irish affability, Korean enthusiasm and Japanese indifference.

Their indifference annoyed me. I liked Niigata. It was my Japanese hometown, and people were calling it names.

'It's a shithole, isn't it?' said the tout affably, and then he said the words that were to become a mantra in Niigata and in Japan over the next few days: 'You wouldn't know there was a World Cup going on here from the atmosphere.'

This was Niigata's moment. It had the honour of hosting the first match in Japan, and only the second match of the first World Cup ever to be held outside Europe and the Americas. For the only time in its history millions of people in Japan and all over the world would have their attention turned to this small port city. Millions of Irish, millions of the Irish diaspora, and millions of English in neighbourly affection would be interested in what was happening here. This was Niigata's moment in the light, and they came close to blowing it.

Niigata is famous for two things: first, for not being atom-bombed during the Second World War. The nearby city of Nagaoka, 20 minutes away by shinkansen across the rice plain, was the back-up target for Nagasaki. It was selected as reserve for nuclear destruction because it was the hometown of Admiral Yamamoto, the man who planned the attack on Pearl Harbor. For being the birthplace of Yamamoto, it had already been bombed flat with conventional weapons, but, because the weather over Nagasaki was fine that day, Nagaoka was ultimately spared. Niigata is famous secondly among seismologists. It was the place where the phenomenon of liquefaction was first observed. Niigata's name means 'new swamp', and until modern times the streets of Niigata were a network of canals. During the great Niigatan earthquake of 1964, some of this reclaimed land started to act as if it were a fluid. The Niigatans were the men who

KICKING

built their houses on the sand, and when catastrophe came, the buildings tilted like boats on the shore. So Niigata is famed as the place where the air does not turn into fire, but where the earth will turn into water: neither choleric nor sanguine, the atmosphere there moves from melancholic to phlegmatic. It is also twinned with Hull.

Although on an England map overlaid on Japan Niigata would be in the approximate position of Liverpool, the city's authorities had good reason for developing links with Hull. Niigata sits on the mouth of a major river, has a port orientated towards the country's cold and dull northern neighbours, and, in the shinkansen, an expensive transport link of questionable utility. Hull was the obvious choice.

The comparison doesn't work in Niigata's favour. Its transport link of questionable utility was a bullet train to Tokyo rather than just a bridge to Scunthorpe, and the shinkansen line pumps a dose of metropolitan adrenalin straight into the heart of what would otherwise be one of the sleepiest regions of Japan. The shinkansen was commissioned by another of the region's famous sons, 1970s prime minister Kakuei Tanaka, and its usefulness has always been questioned by the other Japanese, but never by the Niigatans. The city would never have been chosen as a World Cup venue if it hadn't existed.

I spent the day at the station chatting to the arriving Irish and the ticket touts. Gradually the tulip tubs, the nearest containers available, filled up with beer cans and cigarette ends. Some of the tulips got crushed when the barrels were used as seats. There weren't enough bins and there were no benches. The ticket touts had a sideline in selling pins specially made for this event, pin money that amounts to a lot more than pin money. The Irish came up to look at the pins and chat, the younger ones quick to agree with the shithole assessment. An old boy in green, huge and with a gait that was ponderous from age and weight, trundled up.

'Look at this old paddy,' said one of the touts with sympathy. 'It's a long way to Tipperary,' he added when the old boy got within earshot.

But he had said it with too much lilt, and despite his affability, the old paddy bridled at the jibe. But he was a businessman, this ticket tout, and he quickly restored the old man's mood and even sold him a pin, 'Made specially, you won't get them anywhere else.'

There was an odd German man wandering around the station who claimed to be the head of the referees. He was very imprecise for a

German referee and manager, and something about his tubby shape and his rambling story about his circuitous journey through Japan (he had decided not to take the direct route to Ibaraki where he claimed the referees were gathering) did not ring true. An English lad biked up with an equally incredible but more believable story. He claimed to be from Leeds originally but his accent was unplaceable. He had been in Niigata for many years and worked on the docks. This put him in a category of his own in a country where almost all the foreigners in parochial towns would be English teachers. This docker was preoccupied with his Japanese wife's infidelity and the manner of its discovery, and you could not blame him for it was odd, and I heard him telling the same story a number of times over the next few days. He told the ticket tout and then me in succession, how it was a stain of his wife's menstrual blood that had alerted him to her betrayal. He said 'menses', a term that I had never heard anyone utter before. The stain appeared on their sofa while a male friend of his had been staying at their house, and perhaps by its positioning or its timing or by her reaction to his discovery, this stain told him that his friend and his wife had slept together. He was understandably hurt and had determined to divorce her. They had settled the split in millions of yen.

I asked, missing my own children, if he had kids. He did.

'You'll miss them,' I said.

'It was her doing.'

Someone asked him where the brothel was.

The cuckolded docker told him, and pointed to a road just down from the station, and the price: three hundred pounds.

'Three hundred pounds for a fuck,' he said, amazed that anyone should have to pay that much for sex. But the same thing had cost him thousands.

The ticket tout told his own tale of how he met the Emperor. It was during the Nagano Olympics, an event, he said, to which the touts were welcomed because they enabled people to get tickets when the system had failed. The Emperor, surrounded by bodyguards, passed the tout from London. The tout, with British insouciance, shouted 'Hello!' over the heads of the bodyguards, and the Emperor replied, 'Welcome to Japan.'

So, I was underwhelmed by Niigata when the Irish were there that first day, and disappointed. I had harboured an affection for this town for a decade. It was the first place I lived after graduating from university. It was where I found I missed my student girlfriend so much that I invited her to come and live with me. It was where we had left from to go back to England for our wedding, and it was where we first lived together as a young married couple. She was from Grimsby originally; she had come 7,000 miles to be with me, only to end up in a town that was twinned with Hull.

This was ten years ago, at the height of the Japanese boom. Money was everywhere and work was undemanding. I, along with thousands of other new graduates from the West, had been invited over to team-teach English in Japan's junior and senior high schools.

Team-teaching was a pedagogical technique invented by the Japanese Ministry of Education in which a Japanese teacher of English and a native English speaker took joint responsibility for lessons. The Japanese teacher would be in charge of explaining the grammar, maintaining order, and for fitting the lesson into the curriculum, while the native English speaker would take responsibility for smiling. Occasionally I would also be called on to read the textbook or ask the kids if they liked baseball.

Team-teaching didn't involve me in any teamwork, or indeed any teaching, so it was a grand misnomer. And for many experienced teachers it must have been galling to pretend to be the equal of an untrained Westerner, barely out of school, whose only contributory skill was the ability to speak a language he had learned as a two year old. Most Japanese teachers accepted this unequal division of responsibilities with good grace, but, like the rare occasions when you are treated badly in Japan, it isn't the good grace you remember. The teachers you remember were the ones who had the character to stand up to this charade.

In one of the suburbs of Niigata city I team-taught with an idiosyncratic but gifted teacher called Chiaki Watanabe who had no intention of letting some unqualified, stripling male into her classroom without letting him know who was in charge.

We had a civilised encounter, Chiaki and I. No sex, no violence, just an elegant human relationship that was not without affection, but not without friction. It was Japanese lady-blossom versus English fop over the tea things.

As I had fair hair and was good at smiling, and was better at English than anyone for miles around (and with Mrs Watanabe contributing the discipline, the lesson plans, and the *esprit de classe*), it wasn't long before I began to rival her for popularity with the kids. This was a mistake. As soon as she realised that I was riding piggyback on her to the school's English-teaching wall of fame, she took preventative action. She left me in the middle of a lesson.

I was faced by forty 13 year olds, the extent of whose functional command of English exactly matched the extent of my functional command of Japanese: an ability to say, and reply to, the words 'good morning'. We stared at each other, and then at the door through which Mrs Watanabe had disappeared, both sides hoping that she was about to come back. She didn't. We said good morning to each other a few times. I looked down at the lesson plan which Mrs Watanabe had thoughtfully provided and decided to try to carry on in the best English tradition of *Carry On*.

When she came back 20 minutes later, it was obvious from the relief on all of our faces that, whatever team-teaching meant, in reality I was her *assistant*. While for her part, she had the sort of smile on her lips that real teachers have when a troublesome pupil has learned an important lesson.

But reminding me of how much I depended on her wasn't enough. Raising her game, she decided one break-time to instruct me in the traditional Japanese etiquette for using a cup and saucer. As I suspected that these weren't ancient Japanese drinking utensils, and that they might owe something to European, and specifically British, influence, I decided to ignore this sally. Her next gambit was more ambitious. She challenged me to a game of chess. Having already proved that she was a better teacher than I was and more adept with European crockery, I wondered how good she could possibly be.

The game was at her flat. As she was widowed, she invited a much younger female colleague along as a chaperone, although anyone who might have seen the two of them would have assumed their roles were reversed. We ate, and during the meal Mrs Watanabe told me about the punishment she had meted out to the last European who had taken her on. She had invited her victim out to dinner, and, having thought long and hard about what would be the least appetising dining experience that Japan could offer a European, she decided on a restaurant that served nothing but eels. Unfortunately her guest looked at the menu and said, 'But I love eels!' and Mrs Watanabe was forced to shell out for a dining companion in whom she had failed to induce vomiting. This must have been galling for her, but it was obviously one of her favourite anecdotes. The meal she served me that night was utterly unmemorable, which means it must have been edible.

After dinner we set the chessboard up. At my level, you can tell a lot about a chess player from the way they set the board up. Do they put the pieces in the correct order? Do they put the board the right way round (with a white square on the extreme right of the nearest row)? Do they put it the right way up? If they get all three right you know you might be in trouble.

The first thing I noticed about Mrs Watanabe's level was that she didn't know how to set the board up. This was an excellent start, though I was suspicious that it could be a feint to make me over-confident. But, as we moved from the opening into the middle game, it became obvious that Mrs Watanabe could not play chess. She wasn't bad. She didn't stop in the middle of a move to check that she was moving her knight properly. She didn't over-expose her queen or slap her head and cry 'but I didn't see that' when I took a piece. But she was undoubtedly going to lose.

I duly won, and then I did something that I had never been able to do before or repeat since. I recreated the position of the pieces on the board at a key stage in the game and showed her where she went wrong. I didn't crow, but we both knew what had just happened: Mrs Watanabe had been bested. After the game she produced an after-dinner sweetmeat for me to try: a jar of char-grilled grasshoppers. They had the taste and texture of roasted coffee beans.

Japan's record of relations with the West has not been as sweet as my relationship with Mrs Watanabe. The team-teaching programme was both an explicit attempt to get Japan to internationalise and, by having them spend a couple of well-paid post-graduation years here, an implicit attempt to get more Westerners to understand Japan. The scheme was called the Japan Exchange and Teaching (JET) Programme and is still running, one of a long line of attempts by Japan to reconcile itself with the existence of the West.

The first attempt lasted for over 200 years and the Japanese strategy was to refuse to have anything to do with us and hope we would go away. This ended in 1853 when the Americans, needing ports in South-east Asia, forced the country to open up by demonstrating their overwhelming technical and military superiority with warships that were steam-driven into the middle of Tokyo Bay. This was such a shock to Japan's isolationist government that it collapsed. The new government, under the catchy but politically and factually incorrect slogan 'expel the barbarians', then invited in as many barbarians as it could to help them catch up with the West.

This second strategy involved Japan learning from the West, but the rapid technical advances did not keep pace with any development towards modernity in the country's civil institutions, and militarism and extreme nationalism became dominant. During the Second World War, Japan's actions in places outside its borders – Pearl Harbor, Nanking, Burma – became synonymous with barbarism for all the countries they affected.

After the atom bomb had demonstrated once more America's overwhelming technical and military superiority, Japan adopted a third strategy. Having re-established itself as an economic rather than a military power, the Japanese state once more began to invite foreigners in. But this time, instead of wanting to learn from them, they wanted to teach them about Japan. The 1964 summer Olympics in Tokyo, and the winter Olympics in Sapporo in 1972 and Nagano in 1998, were all opportunities to show Japan to the world. The JET Programme was similarly conceived. But the real prize was the 2002 World Cup.

So what happened on the streets of Niigata in those early days mattered. None of my negativity towards the city was based on an independent discovery of the truism that you cannot recover the past by revisiting a place. It wasn't the remembered excitement of youth, easy work, easy money and love life with a loved wife that made this occasion so staid in comparison, it was the awareness that the Japanese didn't seem to have realised that they needed to embrace the World Cup, and not divert themselves around it as the Niigatans seemed to be doing. They had to do more than just provide the infrastructure and organisation while leaving the foreign fans to create the atmosphere.

Providing their own atmosphere was something the Irish have never had difficulty doing. That night up in a small dark faux-British pub called the Black Pig in the centre of the old town, the Irish chanted and sang, and had drank the owner out of beer and glasses by midnight. He had been told to expect only about 150 Irish in the city that night, and just like the authorities he was unprepared for the many hundreds who had arrived. He only had a dozen or so Guinness glasses to cope with the scores of Irish who were packed into the pub and spilling onto the pavement outside.

In the pub were the ticket touts, a local television crew and a few brave besuited Japanese businessmen who would have stories they could tell to the next two generations about the night they braved the possibility of hooliganism and sang and chanted with the Irish in the Black Pig.

'They fucking love it, don't they?' said the tout. 'That's the thing with the Japanese: they like to buy atmosphere.'

Round the corner at another gaijin bar called Blockeys, bigger than the Pig and with pool tables, the same thing was stated with less pragmatism and more mysticism by the head of the Cullen family (two brothers and three sons) who had been doing the temples down south the day before.

'It's like we're ghosts wandering through Japan for all the notice they take of us,' he said. 'It's fine for them, but . . .'

His brother told me about an Irish pub back in Tokyo's Roppongi which, because of the English presence nearby, was surrounded at night by the police. They had made plans to meet there the next night, but hearing about the tension had made them change their minds. So it was that they missed the Irish choir on the steps above Paddy Foley's and would never see the signs that said 'PLEASE MOVE' and 'BE QUIET'.

Also in the bar was one of the two Japanese-speaking foreigners the Niigatan prefectural government had taken on specifically to cope with the demands of the World Cup. He was a resident of one of Niigata's other sister cities, Illinois. The American was corn-fed, well bred, but no soccer-head. He admitted he knew nothing about football, and it did not seem to have occurred to him or his bosses that enthusiasm for, or any knowledge of the game might come in useful when preparing for the arrival of tens of thousands of the world's football fans. Niigata's relationship with Illinois was more important than that.

Later that night, as I went home, I saw little groups of Irish wandering up through an almost empty city looking for that atmosphere that wasn't there.

The next day was better, however. First the kamikaze, the god wind, had blown away the cloud, and Niigata was bright and fresh in the morning air. There were meeters and greeters in bright yellow on the station forecourt and in the old town, and in the shopping district near to the station a small Astroturf five-a-side pitch had been laid out on the open square of a first-floor shopping mall. Here a local Japanese team played impromptu barefoot games with scratch teams of enthusiastic Irish. The Irish with their years of experience were good at dogged defence and feinting attacks, the Japanese with their traditions of flexibility and agility had better and flashier individual skills. A Japanese lad played keepy-uppy for about a minute as he was harried by one of the lads who had pronounced Niigata a shithole – he was enjoying himself now. On the road below a Irish girl who lived in Niigata had got the use of a car and was driving round the town blaring her horn and swinging a tricolour from the window.

As I watched the barefoot football a Japanese journalist for a sports paper asked to speak to me.

'Do you know fooligan?'

It was the first question he asked me when he learned I was English.

Further along in the bright sunshine, a BBC journalist was interviewing a fan who had dyed his hair such a fluorescent shade of green that you wondered for the health of his head beneath such powerful chemicals.

'There are more of you here than us,' he said of the journalists, 'put that in your report.'

And indeed later that night outside the Black Pig, as the Irish swilled and milled and spilled, there were at least five photographers waiting for whatever it was they expected to happen.

As I wandered around I bumped into three lads I had directed earlier to a gaijin bar called, with sensitivity, Immigrants, which I had told them was opposite the post office. Yet here they were, ten minutes walk from the post office, being led further away from it by an old man in the bright yellow of a volunteer uniform.

'I think you're going the wrong way,' I said.

'We're thinking that too.'

Immediately I knew I was in the sort of situation that Japan gets you into. Here was an old man, easily in his 60s, though being Japanese he could have been 80, he had given up his time to help the foreigners in his city, he was walking them, as somehow was established though he didn't speak English, to a post office. It was a long way, a good 15-minute trek in the hot sunshine, but instead of just directing them he was prepared to lead them there. Unfortunately he was leading them the wrong way, not to the closest post office but to the main one in the centre of the old town. Now whatever I did I was going to humiliate him in front of these three foreigners, me, a young man with appalling Japanese. I was about to tell him that he had made a mistake, and undoubtedly in front of these three lost foreigners he was going to have to turn round and take them back the way they had come. There would be no way he would be able to disguise his error because they would be retracing their steps. And for a second, actually for a few seconds, I thought it would be better to let this old man save face than it would be to let the three Irish go to the bar they wanted to (which was probably closed at that time of the day anyway). But they knew they were going the wrong way, and now I was involved, and I didn't have the Japanese to explain this with any subtlety.

'*You're wrong way!*' I said to the old man. '*These foreigners to front-of-station post office want to go. Opposite front-of-station post office there is bar, they want to go to that bar. I'm sorry, I apologise, but you're wrong way.*'

The old man was understandably reluctant to accept what I was saying.

'*But there's a perfectly good post office up there. It's the main post office, that's where they asked to be taken.*'

I hated myself for doing this, and I acted like the man I would see later on the train to Sendai. I narrowed my shoulders and dropped my head down in an attempt to be obsequious and Japanese. And then, bizarrely to both of us, I used a gesture which I did not even know was Japanese. I held out my hands together as if I was praying and bowed.

'I am so sorry for my rudeness,' I said.

I had seen the Japanese do this, but only as a blessing for dinner and in front of shrines, and I simply had no idea if this was a gesture that is used as an apology. I didn't even know from where I had picked it up. To him I might have been doing the equivalent of blessing him with a full Catholic cross, all spectacles, testicles, wallet and watch.

'No, honest, they want to go to the front-of-station post office.'

Reluctantly he turned round and led his charges back the way they had come. Foolishly I called after him words that probably compounded his humiliation.

'I'm sorry. I apologise. Sorry.'

Up in the old town the Irish were beginning to feel the first touches of Japanese warmth. 'Everyone has been so lovely,' said Colne and Angela, an Irish couple munching a fruit-filled crepe suzette (the only food they were prepared to risk at this early stage). 'They're so kind and helpful, nothing's too much trouble.'

And this was all I heard now; all the shithole talk had gone.

I went into the Black Pig to see how the night before had gone.

'Any problems?' I asked the owner, who I think was British but who, like the docker, had been in Japan so long that his accent was unidentifiable.

'None, they were brilliant, so well behaved. The police drove up when we were closing up and stared us out but otherwise nothing. Except somebody took a skull that I was using as a bog-brush holder in the toilet; I hope they're not using it as a mug.

'They went crazy last night,' he added, as he unpacked a supply of plastic glasses. 'Last night I did four kegs of Sapporo when the most I have ever done before is one. Tonight and Saturday will be the biggest nights Niigata has ever had, but we're ready for it now. Yesterday took us by surprise a bit.'

But at midnight he had run out of drink again. The Irish stayed on the street happily drinking cans of lager, singing 'Come on you Boys in Green' and milling on the street with not a policeman in sight. But the streets of Niigata were empty of Japanese. It was Friday night in Niigata and ten years ago I remember the streets of the old town being full of people partying. But whether it was due to the recession or the fear of hooliganism was impossible to tell.

KICKING

On this second night there were a few more Japanese, and they were different from the friends of gaijin and anecdote collectors who had been there the night before. The very strangeness of the Irish presence had brought out the alternative crowd, the small percentage of Niigatan youth who dye their hair to copper, and who are looking for something other than conventional family and salaried life. They are usually too cool to care about foreigners, particularly as most of the foreigners in Niigata are teachers working for the school system that most of them have rejected. But here they were, using the terrible English that they had sneered at their more conventional conscientious cousins for learning, and excited by this disturbing element that had arrived in their town.

On the day of the game the first thing that hit me as I came onto the station forecourt was the smell of beer that wafted from the sweat of a thousand Irish gathered there, from the hundreds who had stayed in the city and from those who had come up from Tokyo for the day. There was a gang of lads dressed in full leprechaun costume attracting all the amateur and professional cameramen, but the essence of Ireland was stout distilled through a million sweat glands into the very air.

One of the dozens of ticket touts moved through the crowd whispering 'ticket' from the side of his mouth, trying to move inconspicuously, aware of the police but obviously doing business. But not so obviously to two Japanese housewives. He whispered 'ticket' and held up two fingers in the English victory gesture, meaning two ten-thousand yen notes, but this is also the Japanese finger sign for peace, and thinking that this was all part of the intercultural carnival the two housewives flashed the sign back to him, and for a moment he thought he had made a deal.

I watched the game in the Black Pig. There was a Brummie woman of Irish ancestry left stranded by her husband and her other menfolk while they took their tickets to the match.

'I made them promise,' she said. 'I told them I would come if the hotel we stayed in had a pool where I could relax while they went to the games. But it doesn't. And now they've left me here.'

If she had been angry she wasn't now, but there was just a touch of nervousness about her being sat in a bar on her own in a country she did not know with some men she did not know. But she was there and was quickly at her ease. We were a motley crew: me; an English journalist working for one of the press agencies; Alex, a tall confident ex-pat Niigata resident in an England shirt who worked for an import–export company; his mate, a law student on his sandwich year studying Japanese law at Niigata University; the cuckolded docker; and his mate, an Israeli with long hair. We had seats and a few Irish drifted in accompanied by the ubiquitous film crew, but apart from them, we were not rapt by the screen and the talk turned, as it always did those first few days, to hooliganism.

The cuckolded docker told the story about how he helped an Englishman change some money. In return for the favour the Englishman showed him the flag he had prepared for the Argentine game. It had 'Come on England' on the front and 'We've got the Falklands' on the back.

'It's you I'm worried about,' Alex said with confident censoriousness to the docker. Clearly he thought him a hooligan.

'No, not me,' said the docker, but he was uncomfortable.

Unfortunately his Israeli companion chose this moment to chip in.

'What about that thing you were telling me,' he laughed, 'about when you were deported from Israel, some United match?'

But he was shushed with whispers and dampening gestures that were almost comic.

'I don't want my country's name dirtied,' said Alex firmly. 'Be the gentleman.'

'Not me, nothing like that,' and he didn't say 'governor', but he may as well have.

After the match it rained, and despite all the owner's preparations and protestations the Black Pig ran dry again. The fans spilled onto the street under the awning and spread out on the covered side streets. As I stood across the road from them under the opposite cover, a woman joined me. She was in denim with a flowery shirt and was perhaps in her late 40s, and I knew she was unmarried. I knew just from her clothes and the fact that she was there at all.

The Japanese women I knew had a femininity that is divided into four jerky but discrete stages. And like the Japanese generally, they moved instantly from one state to another, without, it seemed, any smearing of the self as it left old habits behind and took up new ones. They started in schoolgirl purdah: their navy-blue tops and jet-black

KICKING

109

hair concentrating the eye on their unmade-up faces, a trick which curiously emphasised their individuality over both their femininity and their uniformity. By the time they got to college, they had reverted to identikit toddler cute: cartoon animals all over their clothes and in their hair. They squeaked, they simpered, they giggled. Yet, despite their age, when I used to be around these babes I never felt lucky. In fact I felt like a pervert. Of course, some men liked their Japanese women this way, mostly Japanese men, although there were a few Westerners who were fooled into thinking that this was their permanent persona. Next, they graduated on to becoming Miss Girl-about-town. They had jobs and boyfriends, exquisitely tailored two-piece suits and to-squeak-for accessories. But they were only illustrations in lifestyle magazines come to life, and, for all their cosmopolitan trappings, this stage in their lifecycle was a false flowering of independent adulthood. The couture was a cover beneath which they became a wife.

Japanese women snapped into being a Japanese wife with heartbreaking speed. In the West being married is a process, but in Japan it is a state of being, and that state is an unhealthy realism. There was no slow dawning of disillusionment after the honeymoon years as there can be in the West. Japanese women seemed to master all the contradictory reactions a woman can have to marriage between saying 'I' and 'do'.

Much of the time I lived in Japan I was stuck for female Japanese company. It was Goldilocks and the four black-haired bears: one was too young, one too cute, one too groomed, and the other too fierce. It wasn't until I discovered older unmarried Japanese women that I found one who was just right.

Many Japanese think they are mad, but the women who had avoided matrimony or who had reconciled themselves to spinsterhood didn't seem mad to me. They took their careers seriously; they could afford to travel abroad; the time that they saved alternately pandering to and then panning their husbands could be spent on pursuing their own interests; and what to a Japanese could be written off as old-maid madness just looked like individuality to me. Old maids everywhere are portrayed as grotesques, but their independence made them seem like Western women to me.

This one, however, was odd.

We listened as the lilting melody of 'Gary Lineker is a wanker, is a wanker' came drifting through the drizzle to us.

'English hooligan drink, dance, have fun from morning,' she said.

She said hooligan, but she meant fan. She said English, but she meant Irish.

I had no idea where this was going so I just agreed.

'Japanese people would sleep if they did that. English people very high level [at drinking].'

I asked her what was she was doing standing there in the rain watching the Irish.

'Nothing.'

As I was still taking notes, she asked me what I was doing standing there in the rain watching the Irish. Was I a journalist? Writer I said. Across the road at least two television crews were interviewing the fans.

Behind us two young Japanese women were watching all these loud young men with interest. An elderly couple passing by realised the source of the noise and the man let out a whoosh of realisation and surprise.

'Movie writer?' the unmarried woman asked. 'Did you write *Eternal Love?*'

'No.'

'Japanese young lady troublemaker,' she said of the girls. 'In Tokyo happy-happy, in Niigata first kiss is look.'

I didn't get her meaning, quite.

'I am cool,' she explained.

'Yes, you are.'

But once again I had failed to understand her.

'Young lady, hot hot hot.'

'Yes, nice to meet you. Bye bye.'

Round the corner at the entrance to Blockeys a fat American was shovelling fried noodles into his mouth.

'I have never heard of this town before,' he said, 'and I am not a typical American who knows nothing about geography. I like geography and I've never heard of it.'

As he was American I told him it was famous for not being atom bombed because of Pearl Harbor.

'Just retribution?' he asked disapprovingly and I couldn't make up my mind whether just meant only or justified.

I told him about Admiral Yamamoto. But he knew his history. He even knew that Yamamoto was assassinated under the orders of the President. The Americans had cracked the Japanese code and knew where his plane would be so they sent one of their own to take him down. This was controversial because targeting an individual officer was apparently closer to a war crime than atom-bombing civilians.

'What should I do with my garbage,' he asked having demolished his fried noodles. 'I wouldn't think twice about it in New York, but here everywhere is so clean.'

'There are lots of street cleaners,' I told him, and we compromised on leaving his garbage in the pile outside Blockeys.

I was barhopping back to the station via all the gaijin joints. Outside an American-run bar called Cheers, a solitary Irishman was extolling the courtesy and efficiency of the Japanese, though he could not understand the lack of programmes or announcements in English. He told a story about how 'a young lad – an idiot' had kicked a hole in his hotel room wall, and how his roommates had made him go down to the front desk and apologise in case they were branded hooligans. So Japan had got him too.

I crossed the bridge over Niigata's narrower version of the Humber for what I believed could be the last time. The neon was flashing off the drizzle in the air, off the river and off the shimmering tarmac, and I remember it being said that Piccadilly Circus would be beautiful if you couldn't read. I couldn't read here, and it made Japan beautiful. Down by the riverside a traffic attendant, his staff and jerkin flashing like a light sabre, controlled the traffic in front of a warehouse party that had been organised to welcome the Irish.

At last, on the night after the game, Niigata finally came good. It was huge, this party by the river. You could watch highlights of the Germany v. Saudi Arabia game, dance, mix your Guinness with sake, or watch Irish lads and Japanese girls flirting and chatting each other up in a way that made you realise how good a World Cup could be when the atmosphere is right. The only thing was, it wasn't official. It had been organised by the foreign residents who had been the only people in the city to realise exactly what was needed.

I got to the station to take the romantically named Echigo

Moonlight train to Tokyo so that I could see England play Sweden. There was a grim-looking policeman watching the forecourt.

'*Excuse me*,' I said, '*Irish people. How was it? OK?*'

'*OK.*'

Then he thought for a moment.

'Gentlemen,' he said.

NIIGATA PART TWO

England 3 Denmark 0
13–16 June

BUT NOT ALL THE IRISH WERE GENTLEMEN.

It is two weeks later, and two days before England's second-round game against Denmark. I am back in Niigata again. As I check in, I am handed this:

For Hotel Guests
Special Notice

Thank you for stay in our Hotel.
For some reasons, we would like you to understand following matters in advance.

3. The refrigerator is rock in the room.
* Please use the vending machine on the 5 to 12 floor.
4. Stop the outside line on your room telephone.
* Please use the public telephone on the 4th floor.
5. Pay TV dose not work.
6. No massage service.
7. No laundry service.

We are sorry inconvenient.
NIIGATA WASHINGTON HOTEL
Manager

'*Why?*' I ask the desk clerk.

'*In the last couple of weeks we have had a lot of foreigners staying who unfortunately forgot to pay before leaving.*'

'*That's too bad.*'

'*Yes it is. Are you happy with the conditions? Please accept our apologies.*'

'*No problem.*'

As I walk out of the hotel there is a notice. 'Policeman dropping in place. Police doing patrol on the every time.'

Niigata is nervous and quiet. In Cheers it is just five ex-pats lining the bar.

'They're worried that the English are going to lose here,' says one barfly. 'They haven't lost yet.'

'I know.'

'Heck, I'm a bar owner,' says the bar owner, 'and I'm worried.'

The Black Pig is busier. But the owner too has concerns. He has been with the police for four hours that day to reassure them. It is no longer the affable Irish. This time the Black Pig is packed and panting with Englishmen getting slaughtered, ready to send home the Danish.

A Japanese man with long lank hair is handing everyone a yellow sheet of photocopied A4. He does not look like the other Japanese in the pub. He lacks their look of eager amazement, and his slight drunkenness is intense rather than helpless. This is his handout.

To The People visiting Niigata for World Cup Succor Game

Welcome to Niigata!

I hope great activity of England Team in World Cup Succor Game.

I am a Japanese barrister and pleads Mr. John Jones's case.

Mr. John Jones, a visitor from England, was arrested because he sold only one ticket for the game between Ireland and Cameroon around the Niigata stadium to a passer-by on June 1st 2002, and still forced to stay in the police station. How amazing it is!

Although he admits his guilty and apologizes, and also tells to pay a fine anytime, Mr. Jones is forced to stay in the police station and have a interview strictly. He is not permitted seeing his family. His health condition is worse, and he suffers from diarrhea blood mixing with.

I guess all Englishmen are very surprised at this story. Under the Japanese criminal system, a defense counsel is not permitted attending at having a interview at the police station, and the suspect is forced to detain for 23 days longest and have a interview strictly in a closed room. While it is said that Japan is an advanced nation, Japan is a savage country at the point of criminal proceeding, so The United Nation advises an inhuman treatment under the criminal proceedings in Japan.

The proceedings of disclosure of the reasons for detention (Habeas Corps) are hold in Niigata District Court with an interpreter on Friday June 14 2002. It is hold in open court, so you, of course, can attend and hear argument there. The mass media will visit the court.

The more visitors, the more the authorities may feel pressure. Mr. John Jones will be released sooner. Come on to the court and help Mr. John Jones.

Barrister Akira Takashima

There is a map at the bottom of the sheet with the faux pub and the real court marked, the route between them inked-in in a staggering line, and the time – 3 p.m. – handwritten twice. But everything else on the map is in Japanese or an alien set of cartographic symbols: the post offices' capital Ts with bars above, the anticlockwise swastikas of the shrines. But if you did not know Niigata, or you could not interpret the Japanese symbols, then the map was nearly useless.

'Are you going to go then?' I ask a couple sat on stools by the bar. The woman responds, but her man does uncommunicative and dour with a panache that is beyond words.

'It's interesting. Yes, we might go. He's English, we should support him.'

'And what do you think about this?' I ask a man standing beside them who seems to be listening. Unfortunately he turns out to be illiterate.

'What is it? I can't read,' he says with just enough challenge to say that I should be careful about my reaction. 'I'm not joking.'

The woman and I begin to give him a précis of the information, but he loses interest.

KICKING

'Is the guy handing out the leaflet the lawyer?'

'Yes,' she says, 'but I hope he'll have sobered up by tomorrow.'

Akira Takashima, the lank-haired lawyer and leafleteer, is now sitting beside me at the bar, writing in the route and the time on more copies of his handout.

'Is this you? Akira Takashima?'

'Yes,' he says too loudly, 'I am famous lawyer.'

At the time I thought it was vanity, but now I suspect he meant he was notorious.

Apart from the hair, which is lank enough, but too long for a Japanese professional, there is something else unusual about him: he is drunk and he is alone, a combination which I have never seen before in Japan. As I talk to him, twice he reaches to take my plastic glass of Guinness, not with a drunken lurch, but with the semblance of one.

'Could I talk to you about this?'

'Yes,' again he is too loud. 'Please translate!' he commands the waitress, even though he has understood what I have said.

The young woman behind the bar smiles willingly and I know she has a little English, but, if the lank-haired Takashima wrote the leaflet, I suspect he might have a little more.

'I was hoping to take Mr Takashima somewhere quieter,' I say, which stretches her English and, in the crowded bar, her hearing beyond its capacity.

Mr Takashima carries on with what he is doing, concentrating hard on inking in the route from the courthouse to the Black Pig.

There is a long silence.

'*I can speak some Japanese,*' I say.

This is truthful, but only so long as Mr Takashima avoids anything that isn't to do with food, shopping and taxis.

'Ah yes,' he booms, 'then please come.'

He leads me out of the packed and tiny Black Pig. Next door there is a small multi-storey car park with seats for its customers by the office. We sit down, I offer him a cigarette that, again in an unprecedented act for a Japanese, he accepts, and which in an ungracious moment annoys me.

He is Akira Takashima, barrister and chief in criminal process in the Niigata Bar Association, but this is the only fact I get from him of which both he and I are completely confident. A combination of his

English, his drunkenness and my Japanese create incoherence, particularly with pronouns. He has seen the suspect, John Jones, two or three times, and once an English business lawyer from Tokyo visited him. He was very surprised by the savage criminal process and very angry apparently.

'Savage,' says Mr Takashima two or three times with passion, referring to the Japanese criminal justice system, or perhaps to the name of the lawyer. 'He should have been freed in 48 hours like England but the prosecutor pushed for the full 22 [23? 24?] days.'

His grandfather was Irish, Mr Takashima explains, which accounts for his being an Ireland supporter. He had a spare ticket because his friend was unable to come to Niigata having been drinking-over. I am unsure what this phrase means, perhaps a combination of over-drinking and staying over. The ticket was sold to a Japanese man who was very happy to buy it. John Jones has two (one? three? four?) brothers and a friend in Tokyo.

So the next afternoon at two I take a bus up to the administrative area of town. I am so early because, foolishly, I believe that there is some possibility that hordes of English may turn out to support their fellow countryman in this alien land. The courthouse is somewhere near the city government offices, which are housed in a tall building in pink pastel that reflects better on the city than the prefectural government offices on the other side of town do on the prefecture. That building, though vast, is squat, solid, unpretentious and grey like the prefecture it organises. But as I pass the city offices, it reminds me of the lurking fear and uncertainty that surrounds any involvement with officialdom in Japan. All foreigners in Japan are required to carry their passport or a gaijin card which had to be renewed yearly.

'Do you mind the gaijin card?' one of my Japanese colleagues had once asked me on one of our annual trips to renew the card. I didn't. 'Because some people resent it,' he added.

'It's your country,' I said casually. 'It's up to you how you run it.'

Later I found out what he meant. It was not just short-stay Westerners like me who were required to carry the gaijin card. The Japanese state also required Korean immigrants to carry one, and not just the newly arrived. The children and even the grandchildren of immigrants, people who did not speak Korean and who had never been to Korea also had to carry the card. This harsh policy accounted for some of the fear, because, even though I was a Westerner and a state employee, though later a freelance teacher, I knew that if anything went wrong I would be within a system which was implacable in its lack of compromise.

For, although the bureaucracy of immigration is always intimidating to non-nationals in whatever country they are in, the peculiarity of the Japanese case was in the contrast between the gentleness and hospitality of the Japanese and the hard machinations of their state.

I find the courthouse from Mr Takashima's map. There are no signs in English to tell me it is the right building, but it doesn't need any. As soon as I see its pragmatic institutional frontage I know what it is. And there are no pressing crowds of protesting English; the place is dead.

The genkan is no longer in use. So in my shoes I step up onto the vinyl flooring and speak to the porter.

'Excuse me, today at three o'clock, a foreigner, a Mr John Jones, is in the court?'

The porter is helpful. He takes me to the scheduling book where John Jones' name is written in the Japanese letters used for foreign words, then he points vaguely at the map on the wall to indicate the courtroom. I ask him again, and this time he is more precise, but he lacks the eagerness to please I have got used to from the World Cup volunteers or the JR staff. As he talks to me, a man whose role I cannot understand walks past and laughs when he hears I am interested in the gaijin. He seems to know the porter, he seems to have a role in this building, and, although Japanese laughter can indicate embarrassment or amusement, as it reverberates down the corridors it sounds to me derisive.

I have half an hour before the case begins so I walk across the road to the park. Here there are shrines, stone lanterns, twisted pines and cobbled paths, all the images of authentic Japan that we gaijin come looking for. But it is the courthouse that is authentic. Not because of the absence of helpful volunteers, nor because of the disused genkan, it is authentic because there is no English. It is very rare to be in any public space in Japan where the presence of English is absent. All the stations, the train announcements, the advertisements, the products, the newspapers, the magazines, even the snatches of overheard conversation contain English. The courthouse was the first place I had seen in which there was no allowance made for internationalisation.

Back outside the courthouse, as promised by Mr Takashima, the mass media are visiting the court. There are several Japanese TV crews and a Danish reporter-cameraman, but no English.

John Jones' brother appears with Mr Takashima. The media mass around him.

'What do you think of what has happened to your brother?'

They have invited him to criticise the Japanese legal system, but he does not fall into the trap. His response is dignified and diplomatic. There is concern all over his face.

The couple from the Black Pig, who it turns out are themselves landlords in York, arrive – Mrs Talkative and Mr Taciturn.

'There's no one else here,' I tell them and we go up to the courtroom together.

It is a utilitarian courtroom based on the Western style, the judge has a raised wood-fronted desk, two tables face each other where the defence and the prosecutor sit, a stenographer or clerk beneath the judge's table, a policeman off to one side, no jury. The brother, the reporters, the York landlords, a couple of Japanese court junkies and me are all behind a railing opposite the judge's bench. It is like a stripped-down church with a raised altar, a choir, a screen between the officials and the ordinary people. There are four doors: one at the back for the judge, one on the defence side for the suspect, one on the prosecution side for the officials, and another for the public.

Four policemen bring John Jones in from the door on the right.

'I'm all right,' he says to his brother and winks.

But he does not look all right. He has grey hair, and a grey beard that is just beyond stubble. He is slightly stooped and wearing something like a grey tracksuit. He is handcuffed and the handcuffs are roped to his waist. The police untie the rope then undo the handcuffs, then they flank him, two either side.

Jones asks, 'Are the press here? Are those the people from the pub?'

The judge enters. We all stand. He waves us, and Jones, to sit back down.

The interpreter is introduced. He is an old man with white hair who, I think, is a retired English teacher. For Japan his translation is adequate, but not adequate enough for Jones' brother. The session starts with biographical details.

'Name? Date of birth? Address?'

Jones gives them the information, but ends his address with a London postcode, NW5, which the interpreter does not seem to understand.

'NW?'

'North-west,' explains Jones.

'North?' hesitates the interpreter.

'North-west,' says the judge, clarifying it for the interpreter. From this first intervention, I sense that the judge has done his work on this case, and probably speaks English.

'Occupation?'

'Jeweller.'

'Joule?' asks the interpreter.

'Jeweller!' says Jones' brother from the public gallery. The interpreter's two mistakes with just the bio-details have made him anxious for his abilities with the more difficult material. He holds up one of his hands and jiggles the ring on it with his other to show the interpreter what is meant. The York landlord also speaks out loudly with a voice that mingles concern with contempt for the interpreter's English.

'Ah, jeweller,' says the interpreter.

The law and the clause under which he is being detained are announced: the Immigration Act under the clause 'to prevent troublesome conduct'. Then the facts of his arrest: at 1.45 p.m. on 1 June at an underground pass around Niigata station he sold a ticket for the Ireland v. Cameroon game to a 33-year-old Japanese man for twenty thousand yen. He was also found to be not carrying a passport. He was arrested therefore for three reasons: for having no fixed address in Japan; for the doubt over his motivation for selling the ticket; for not having a passport on him.

Mr Takashima then begins his attempt to get Jones released. This is not a trial. All that is happening today is that the prosecution has to demonstrate under defence probing that it has sufficient reason to detain Jones while they continue to investigate his crime or crimes.

The four main characters in this event play their parts with dramatic perfection. Jones is, after two weeks in Japanese jail, in a wretched

KICKING

condition. The judge is distinguished and he has smart silver-grey hair that can only come from years of immersion in the law. The prosecutor looks like a bureaucrat, sometimes bored and always unimpressed by the histrionics of the defence. Takashima has a frustrated idealism that has been worn, but not broken, by what I assume is years of working the defence in a country that is prosecution led.

Takashima: 'He does not understand the three articles under which he has been arrested.'

Judge: 'That doesn't matter as he understands the three reasons for his arrest.'

Takashima: 'He has a legal passport now.'

Judge: 'The circumstances of his motivation for selling the ticket are unclear.'

Takashima: 'So ask the prosecution, they know better than we do.'

All of this is from the translation provided to Jones by the interpreter, and it is impossible to know how accurate it is. But two of Takashima's statements seem edging towards contemptuous. He has a legal passport now (so what's the problem?), well, if that's it then ask the prosecutor.

The prosecutor's bored voice indicates that he thinks this process is a waste of his time. It is to him obvious that there is enough material to justify continuing to detain Jones.

'We are here to indicate the reasons for his arrest so there is no need to explain the investigations of the prosecution.'

Takashima: 'I protest.'

Judge: 'My opinion is the same [as the prosecutor's].'

Takashima: 'As to the motivation, we need to know more about it.'

Judge: 'The motivation is the important thing, I think. Motivation includes way of thinking.'

I am afraid I cannot understand any of this; what is the problem with Jones's motivation and what does 'way of thinking' mean?

Takashima: 'I understand his motivation was that his friend [who had a ticket] hadn't been able to come to Japan.'

Judge: 'I have my doubts that this is the sole reason.'

Takashima: 'Explain the necessity of detention. He will pay the penalty. And cannot meet his family members.'

Judge: 'Our thinking is two things. His motivation is not clear. His dwelling is not clear.'

KICKING

I assume he means the dwelling in Japan, and this seems harsh given that none of us have a dwelling in Japan.

Takashima: 'The suspect, if he pays the penalty, should be released.'

Judge: 'The summary order or simple order has not been issued yet.'

Takashima: 'Any other problems with the violation?'

Judge: 'The investigations have not yet been finished.'

Prosecution: 'This [hearing] is just to explain the reasons, we don't have to explain other minor things.'

Takashima: 'That statement is not right. The offences the suspect may have committed minor things which may be important. I insist to release the suspect as soon as possible. Explain when he can be released, whether the suspect will be released or not released. These things should be said.'

Prosecution: 'Two other minor offences exist, but it is not appropriate to discuss at this court today. Just indicate the reason for detention.'

Something here is not being said: the real reason for Jones' detention. The prosecution perhaps has a suspicion or some evidence that Jones has done something more than end up with a spare ticket and forget to carry his passport. But the prosecutor does not have to reveal whatever additional material he has gathered. All he has to do is show the judge that he has sufficient evidence to hold Jones while the investigations continue. Takashima is getting nowhere, and all the prosecution needs to do is continue the mantra.

Takashima changes his approach.

Takashima: 'Do you know the health condition of the suspect?'

Judge: 'I understand he can endure the detention.'

Takashima: 'Not good, in bad condition: haemorrhage from anus.'

The interpreter pronounces anus as *annus* so it takes a moment to understand what is being said.

Judge: 'I didn't inform the haemorrhage.'

Takashima: 'The prosecution can confirm it.'

For the first time the prosecutor looks confused. His other three interventions were scripted, but this calls for caution. He pauses, then collects himself to give a perfect administrative reply.

Prosecution: 'I have heard of it from the suspect, but have not confirmed it. We would have advised the police to go to the doctor's and get appropriate treatment. We have explained this to the suspect.'

Blunted by this, Takashima returns to his attempt to test the case against Jones.

Takashima: 'Can you explain why "troublesome conduct" against the Niigata code? Was the person who bought the ticket "troublesome"?'

I assume he means did the suspect trouble the purchaser of the ticket.

Judge: 'You cannot comment on the context of the evidence.'

Takashima: 'Did the suspect chase around the person who wanted to buy the ticket?'

Here is the first question that the prosecutor answers.

'The suspect was arrested for selling ticket to a Japanese. He didn't block his way or chase him around.'

Takashima: 'Do you have any evidence he tried to sell the ticket to other people?'

Judge: 'The court will not answer that question.'

Prosecution: 'I believe it is not appropriate to explain these questions in this court.'

So, confounded by both the judge and the prosecution, Takashima is reduced to tautology.

Takashima: 'I believe that answer is not appropriate. The reason for detention must include the reasons why he was detained.'

And the prosecution replies with 'the same thing', and, whether he is taunting Takashima for his tautology, or giving a parliamentary answer – I refer my honourable friend to the answer given to the previous question – I do not know.

Finally Takashima attempts to find out what will happen next.

Takashima: 'Last, the limit of detention of suspect is 21 days. Until then, how will the prosecution handle this matter?'

Prosecution: 'Next Friday, we will handle this matter until that day.' This is in a week's time.

Judge: 'Is there any possibility your decision before the 21st?'

Prosecution laconically: 'If it is handled quickly.'

And that is that. No decision is made, but it seems clear that Jones now will be detained for another seven days.

The defence then has ten minutes in which to make a statement, but since he has failed to get anywhere with his interrogation of the prosecutor, it does not seem that he can achieve anything now.

'He was arrested on 1 June,' Takashima begins, 'but is still detained even though he has admitted the offence and apologised and will pay the penalty. His health condition is bad. Many British people will be surprised that lawyers can't attend interviews and that someone can be detained for 23 days. Criminal procedures are still barbarous, and have been advised by the UN to improve. He sold only one ticket and gained only a little profit. Passport is a minor offence and no reasonable reason for detention. The period to investigate should be ten days maximum. Giving them nine more days is shameful. Bad influence will affect the relationship between the UK and Japan.

'The unreasonableness of the detention, it is a very minor thing. He is determined to receive a penalty fine. Because of different legal system, suspect has spoken to defence council of his disaffection with court procedures and [to] international press. In minor offence in UK has to be done in 48 hours, also [in] detention house telephone is installed, and interview investigation recording tape and videotape. Of the possible extension to the 21st, suspect was very disappointed. Five or six hours a day of asking the same questions repeated. "Were you a hooligan six years ago? The photo on your driver's licence and yourself is very different." The 12th and 13th, no investigation. Suspect has lost energy in the heat, and has haemorrhage from the anus, and can only shower twice a week. Suspect not used to Japanese climate. Very severe. Request release as soon as possible.'

The judge is unmoved either by Jones' disaffection with the Japanese legal system or his ill health. Takashima's description of the barbarous nature of the Japanese criminal justice system and the UN's criticism also fail to achieve anything, though of course his comments are for the media and not the judge.

The judge then calls Jones to give a ten-minute statement, and, understandably, he is less interested in creating a scene.

'I came to Japan for the World Cup to see my team Ireland,' he says. 'I put my passport in my hotel in Tokyo like I do in any other country. For the next four or five days I went shopping and sightseeing and enjoyed myself. On 1 June I went to Niigata to see Ireland play Cameroon with my three friends. Albert went to another game and asked me to sell his ticket, not for profit, just to recoup our money. When I got to the game I sold it to a Japanese man for twenty thousand yen. Then I was arrested. I had my driving licence with my photo, my date of birth, and my home address, but the passport was still in my hotel in Tokyo.'

'Passport where?' asks the interpreter, who, independently it seems, wishes to satisfy himself as to the exact location of Jones' passport, and cannot quite believe he left it in a hotel room.

'I told you, I left it in the hotel.'

'Locked?'

'Of course locked,' says Jones with some irritation.

'Since that day,' he continues, 'I have been kept in a police station in Niigata. I told the police I was guilty of not having a passport and of selling the ticket. I have been sick, had the doctor with me twice, and was taken to Casualty in Niigata hospital on the third occasion, losing a lot of blood and having difficulty getting around. After an internal investigation, the hospital gave me four different types of medicine. I can't sleep; I can't eat. I am in a small room . . .' and he holds out his arms to show how small it is '. . . 24 hours a day. There is a hole in the floor for a toilet. There's no running water. I haven't had two showers a week; I have only had two showers since I have been there. I have only changed my underwear twice. They have interviewed me every day for the last 14 days. The interviewing is aggressive, violent and intimidating. In the cell there is nothing, no bed, no table. I have been kept incommunicado, no communication.'

'No bed?' questions the judge.

'You get a bed at nine at night, they bring you a mattress on the floor. There must be codes or standards between England and Japan. I am of good character and have never been to a court in my life. If this had happened to a Japanese man in the UK, he would not have been treated in the same way. I have told the same story every day that I told you. I feel suicidal. The language barrier is very frustrating: no one speaks English. I cannot believe I have been treated this way for such a small crime. I broke the law by selling the ticket and by not having my passport. It wasn't intentional. I was just naïve. I am guilty of both charges. Thank you.'

There is no moment when a decision is made, no gavel or 'take him down', but Jones is led away for another seven days of questioning.

'This is an international incident,' he says loudly as he is taken away.

But it isn't. It is a very national incident.

KICKING

127

As Jones is taken out there is something that in a Japanese court could probably be described as uproar.

'What happened to the Japanese man?' shouts the taciturn landlord from York as we file out. 'You should ask the judge why the Japanese man wasn't arrested.'

This is the bravest thing I have yet seen in Japan. If he had needed any convincing that the Japanese authorities take any transgression seriously, the last hour and a half should have done so. He could not have known what might have been consequences of this contempt of court. But this does not stop him. He asks the question with a loud and British belligerence, and the court with the judge still there is for a moment stunned. Everybody looks at everyone else.

Finally it is the interpreter who, in a voice that suggests he is hurt that it might be thought any different, says, 'the same thing'.

It may be the fog of law, but there is something unclear about all of this. Why has this Englishman with a Welshman's name and an Irish affiliation ended up spending three weeks in a Japanese cell? It seems extraordinary that the Japanese authorities should waste their time on a tourist who left his passport in his hotel through ignorance of the law, who tried to unload a spare ticket and who does not have a fixed address in Japan. The prosecutor revealed there were two other minor matters, but what could be more minor than a forgotten passport? If they suspected him of a more serious crime, and the assumption must be from the judge's doubts about his motivation for selling the ticket that this could be ticket touting, why only Jones? Niigata station on the day of the Ireland match had been thick with touts. If on the day of the first game in Japan the authorities had wanted to show that touting would not be tolerated, why hadn't they arrested them all?

But all this was mere curiosity and puzzlement. I was trying to square a circle, a red quartered flag and a flag with a red dot into some hybrid that made sense to me. The point is this. In England the only people whom it is generally considered acceptable to detain for weeks without charge are terrorists, and some of us even doubt the acceptability of incarcerating people suspected of that. In Japan the same could be done to someone who sold a single ticket, had no passport, and was without an acceptable address.

It is a relief to get out of the court and into the sunshine.

'What do you think of that?' I ask a second English couple who had snuck in late to the courtroom and who both appear to have dressed up for their visit.

'It wasn't unlike a magistrate's court in the UK where the judge just acts as a branch of the prosecution,' says the man.

'Did you know about this passport thing?' his wife asks conspiratorially.

I tell her I did, that I have lived in Japan before, and know how seriously they take making sure that non-Japanese carry identification papers.

'But it wasn't in any of those leaflets we were sent.'

'It was buried away.'

It *was* buried away. At the bottom of the third page of the British government leaflet entitled *Going to the World Cup?* it says: 'Visitors to Japan are committing an offence if they do not have their passport on them at all times – those who are stopped and do not have it on them could be arrested.' What it does not say is that they will be banged up in a tiny cell for 21 days with a hole for a toilet, no furniture, no reading matter and no visitors.

'I haven't got my passport on me,' the woman whispers. 'I'm going straight back to my hotel to get it.'

'Perhaps he was on the dodgier side of life,' says her husband, 'but he didn't deserve that.'

'Well, we know what the Japanese are like from the war,' adds the wife, who could not have been born when the war ended.

'Where are you from?'

'London, but probably a different part of London from that poor chap.'

'NW5.'

'Not so far away then.'

But it is only me, the York landlords, the smartly dressed couple, and Jones and his brother among the English who have had our delight in Japan disconcerted by the events in the courthouse. Everyone else is still in love.

....

Later that day I go to the Internet café, the only one in Niigata. Not only does it offer Internet access at half-hourly rates it also hires out *manga*, and its walls are stocked with paperback-sized editions. At the screen next to me an English accountant is looking up next season's Ipswich fixtures while his Australian fiancée looks on. They are both so impressed with Japan they are thinking of moving here. They have been living in America and are fed up with the country.

'Land of the free?' they snort with contempt. 'Yeah, as long as you have got a photo-ID. They're not even allowed digital phones because they can't be tapped into. And the cops! In the UK or Australia once you're in your 30s you don't worry about the cops, but in America everyone's scared of them.'

'It's the same with the Japanese,' I say, and then I tell them the same thing I say to everybody over the next few days. 'Have you got your passport on you? Never ever get involved with the Japanese authorities.'

In response they tell me a story, how three days ago in Niigata they had seen a taxi bump a bicycle. The bicyclist wasn't hurt; the taxi wasn't scratched; even the bike had survived. Thinking nothing of it they walked on. Forty-five minutes later they passed back that way again. But now there was a crowd and the police were tape measuring the distances in order to file an accident report. The system is like a tsunami. A tiny event triggers an irresistible force that rolls on until it eventually engulfs everybody.

But the rest of the English are still caught up in their love of the Japanese, and it is impossible not to respect their enthusiasm.

'They're brilliant. They have taken us right to their hearts and souls. They love us to bits. Of the five World Cups we've seen this is the best.'

This is from a group of five official England supporters from Tadley in Hampshire who are on the streets of Niigata that night. They have all adopted Japanese nicknames, such as '*Ichiban Hagai*' (The Baldest), '*Ichiban Baka*' (The Stupidest), '*Ichiban Sumo*' (the most suitably built to take part in sumo). They all throw their words into a cacophony of praise, although some are drunker than others.

'It has been nothing like anyone said it would be. They said it would be too expensive, it isn't. They said the Japanese would be terrified of hooliganism, but there hasn't been any. The policing has been so laid-back it's brilliant, no tear-gas; so good that it could change the face of football forever. They said they shouldn't hold the World Cup because they knew nothing about the game, but they are doing such a good job we think they should be asked to host every World Cup.

'They don't know anything about football, but they know a lot about people. They have got the people side right. This sets the standard, but I don't think there's any way Germany will be able to match it. They know Beckham by a mile, then it's Owen. They love it, it's mental.'

And to illustrate their point, they start shouting 'Beckham! Beckham!' Japanese youngsters passing on bicycles pull up out of the darkness and the slight drizzle to join in the chanting, adding 'Nippon!' and 'England!' shaking their hands, congratulating them, and wishing them luck. One even apologises for having a Croatian top on.

'It's great the way they adopt one side or the other. We thought they would be reserved, but they treat us like movie stars outside the games. Generous, we've been given hats, flags, badges. At one pub we gave them our England flag and they immediately put it up behind the bar. We're watching the Japanese game and one of the Japanese is called Suzuki so we call him Yamaha or Kawasaki and the Japanese start laughing and shouting 'Honda, Honda'. I have never known anything like this. It's like a carnival, that's the only word that will do, a carnival.

'There aren't many idiots. The majority of English people never did any harm. It's not a result of treating the English well. It's about the people that are here. You haven't got the feeling that there's some tosser in the bar waiting to cause trouble. But it's also not like Italy: police pushing you onto buses. They let you drink and just stand and watch. They have got this spot on. It's 80 per cent the Japanese and 20 per cent the English who are responsible. It's mad and it's mental. Letting fireworks off, all friendly. I'd put it on a par with a holiday. Forget the football, it's a carnival.'

Later the rainy season arrives in earnest. It is so heavy that it is impossible to cross even ten yards between the covered sections of the streets without getting soaked. In Blockeys, where two weeks before the Cullens had said they had felt 'like ghosts . . . for all the notice they take of us', an Englishman, Mark of Chesterfield, who is sitting with 'Be the gentleman' Alex, extols the Japanese.

He tells his illustrative story, of how he and two of his friends were chatting up a couple of girls in a club. One left, but the other stayed. They were trying to get this girl drunk.

KICKING

131

'Three lads in their 30s and one 22 year old and she wasn't worried. It would never happen in England. Everyone feels so safe here. I feel so safe here. In France, when we played Tunisia in Marseilles, it was scary. Here you can leave a bag in a bar and when you go back to look for it, it's still there.

'It just shows,' he adds, 'that if you apply to hold the World Cup you are not just inviting the teams you are also inviting the supporters and you have to welcome them as well. This is what Japan has done.'

'But why are we so popular with the Japanese?'

'It's because we're so good looking,' says Mark.

'Gentleman image,' chips in Alex.

Next day, the match day, I see an Englishman who has got the gentleman image down to a cup of tea. He is coming out of Niigata station as I am queuing for the bus to the stadium. He wears a blue double-breasted suit and a hat that, though not a bowler hat, is just as stiff and solid. He must be good looking too, or someone finds him so, because with him there is a Japanese woman. They are setting off on a half-hour stroll to the stadium, and he has a tight furled umbrella. It is not raining now, but it could again as it has earlier in the day, though, looking at him, I think he would carry the umbrella anyway.

He is the first dandy I have seen, although I would see more of them later. They are few though, these fans who are prepared to dress themselves as icons of Englishness, and there is no uniformity to them. There was the woman in the crown, the two knights with their child-dragon, and various jesters. They all seemed to be looking for some essence of Englishness which could be distilled, like the Mexican sombrero, or the Brazilian bikini, or the sweat of stout seeping through the green shirts of the Irish, into some identifiable marker of Englishness, identifiable to us and to the fans of other nations. But they were failing to hit that mark. Perhaps it was because in the dandy, the knight, the monarch and the joker, they all circled the image of the gentleman, and the gentleman cannot contrive a passion for anything, let alone football. Of course if they had wanted to dress up as something that would have been identifiable to us and to the other fans as the essence of Englishness in World-Cup-world they should have dressed as comedy hooligans. But no one took that on. Unlike the iconic, ironic and non-violent Vikings, there was always the possibility that the real hooligan might still appear.

But not that night. Everything about it was perfect. It had rained hard during the day but had stopped and the rain had left its moisture in the warm evening air. There was no Niigatan subway ride to disorientate us beneath the city. And there was nothing to be scared of from the Danes. Even Ken and Gemma, whom I met up with before the match, could think of nothing to taunt the Danes with.

'How about "At least we don't vote fascist"?' Ken suggests desperately. This is far below his usual standard, and it takes me a while to realise that it is a reference to the Danish referendum on the Euro.

'Perhaps a bit convoluted?'

We have all the excitement of the first knockout round but no knot of apprehension. Even the hopeless, hopeful signs held up high by the ticketless have risen in originality. 'I want to cheer,' one Japanese lad says, 'please give me chance.' The English bubble out of the shinkansen station and either walk or take a short bus ride to the stadium they have seen hovering like a flying saucer on the near horizon. It is called the Big Swan. It sits on the edge of a lake and instead of rising vertically like a coliseum, its sides curve up, outwards and then inwards, creating a profile that was not unlike, but not that like, a swan with its head tucked beneath its wing. Swan or flying saucer, there is no denying its majesty, its strange profile against the darkening horizon, and its lights dappling on the lake.

We enter through a columned and covered area, on the other side of which there was a moat formed by a weir on a stream that led down to the lake. I go down away from the crowds that are crossing the bridge to the stadium and look out across the city where the neon lights are just coming up into brilliance across the lake. Two policemen on the banks of grass on the other side of the weir watch me lazily as I make my way across the lower bridge and back round to the stadium.

As I pass through the security and baggage check a man just ahead of me is bundled away by the shell-suited police. They move him fast to prevent his mates and other bystanders having the time to make a decision about whether to try and intervene. He is passed through a side gate and because he misses the baggage and security check I cannot see what happens to him. He seems relaxed. 'Uh oh, anything could happen now,' he says nonchalantly, and remembering John Jones I know he is right.

Up on the main level you can see right through into the stadium and the excitement of the lights and the people pulls you in. After the stewardesses have shown me to my seat I see the young lad who hugged me at Sapporo and his mate. I have sat near to them at every game.

'It's him again. Where were you at Osaka?'

'Just down from you, I tried to attract your attention but you didn't notice me.'

'Sorry.'

I go up a couple of seats and chat to them.

'I'm not leaving if we lose,' says the mate. 'I'll support the Japanese.'

They are the same as everyone, utterly impressed by the Japanese.

'This has set the standard,' he says. 'The policing has been marvellous. In Sapporo they just coaxed the lads down from the trees, in Italy they would have beaten them down and anyone watching would have got wound up.'

They must have been less than ten during Italia '90, but perhaps they had been following a club there, or have heard the stories from the other fans.

Further up are Ken and Gemma and below somewhere is Rob, and there are others near about I recognise from the other matches. Some quirk of a computer programme or else a near simultaneous booking of our tickets has kept us all together, even though we are never in quite the same place in relation to the goal at each match. This piece of England in World-Cup-world is starting to feel like home.

Off to our right, the Japanese crowd try to start a Mexican wave. But the English are having no truck with submitting their individualism to this conception of the crowd.

'We don't do the wave,' they shout at the Japanese, 'we don't do the wave.'

Then someone produces a lightweight, over-sized football which is batted up and down the crowd. A big Japanese steward comes and confiscates the ball.

'Boo! Give us our ball back!' we all shout.

For the first time I am on a seat next to the aisle, and across from me are the Japanese crowd. There are a lot of middle-aged mothers with children, and young men and women, and they laugh confidently at the constant battle between our desire for unruliness and the stewards' love of rules. They join in the chants they can understand, and copy the hand gestures in their seats. But during the game their reaction to what happens on the pitch is displayed several seconds later than the aficionados at either end. They are like people who get the joke late.

Once the game is underway, a Japanese lad, all alternative hair and insouciance, spots that there is an empty seat beside me and sidles in. He is utterly thrilled to be in the England section and can hardly keep his happiness to himself, to have left the well behaved and be among the bellicose.

1–0; 2–0; 3–0.

'Svengerland! Svengerland! Svengerland!' we sing. 'He's not Swedish any more.'

We have a one-goal lead, a cushion to that lead, and a cushion on top of the cushion. We are so well protected from being dragged down to earth that we feel as mollycoddled as a child deity. It means we are likely to play Brazil in the quarter-final. There is so much happiness about, that even the thinly supported singing of 'No Surrender' takes on a jaunty English air.

At half-time all the English sit down. Across the aisle all the Japanese stand up to visit the toilets, the smoking areas, and the bars. For them it's an interval, but for us it's a rest.

For the whole of the second half it is English carnival. The game goes on below us but nobody is really watching it anymore.

'Let's all have a disco, let's all have a disco', and we dance in our little foot space in front of the seats.

'Let's all have a conga', and three lines of English take to the horizontal aisles and snake back and forth around the seating with some attempt by the stewards to stop them.

A new-to-me Seaman chant is released for the occasion: 'He's got Seaman. He's got Seaman. He's got Seaman on his shirt, on his shirt.'

There are no chants of 'At least we don't vote fascist'.

It turns out the Japanese lad next to me could not keep his happiness to himself after all, and in a very Japanese acknowledgement of equality and selflessness he has let his mate in beside me and is now standing next to me in the aisle.

The big steward who took our ball away comes down to him.

'Could you go back to your seat please? You are getting in the way of other customers.'

The boy takes not the blindest bit of notice. He does not even acknowledge that the steward has spoken to him, and he does not move. Perhaps it is our presence that gives him confidence, perhaps he is like that anyway, perhaps as a customer himself he is exercising his right to silence. But whatever the reason he is showing the same disrespect for authority as the English he has joined.

Down below us a line of policemen has formed itself across the area between the seating and the goal. One policeman had foolishly failed to diet before presenting himself before the English, and in the line of thin policemen he was a nail that needed hammering down.

'You fat copper. You fat copper.'

They're pointing at him en masse, but he gives no sign in his stance or in his expression that he realises what is going on.

'Who ate all the pies? Who ate all the pies? You ate, you ate, you ate, you ate, you ate all the pies.'

I translate this for the Japanese lad beside me who is looking puzzled.

'*Who ate all the eatable things?*'

They don't have pies in Japan and I can think of no equivalent. Except that sushi is a sort of fish pie in reverse with the meat on the top and the carbohydrate underneath. But 'Who ate all the sushi?' doesn't work for me.

The Japanese lad reacts as if this is the funniest thing he has ever heard: taunting a policeman – a policeman! – for his fatness. He is actually holding his sides with laughter.

The crowd, realising that 'Who ate all the pies?' is probably not going to cross the linguistic-cultural barrier, start, to the same rhythm and intonation as they shout 'Rio!', shouting 'Sumo! Sumo!' and the Japanese lads need no help with this. They are doubling up and looking at each other with tears in their eyes. But the policeman to his credit or perhaps to the detriment of his understanding doesn't show it at all. The invective just bounces off him.

The whistle blows full time.

'We're not going home. We're not going home.'

'Three–nil to the In-ger-land.'

Watching the Japanese crowd watching us I suddenly realise that we are part of the entertainment. Despite the fact that we, like them, have paid to be here, we are far more like the players on the pitch than we are like the Japanese. They are behaving like an audience in the theatre, perhaps for a riotous pantomime performance, but an audience nevertheless. They sit down when the action starts and stand up at the interval. We do the opposite because, although it is easy while in the crowd to forget it, we are performing too. Our performance might feel like normal behaviour to us, but it has taken the Japanese presence to put us into perspective. On the pitch there are the protagonists, and on either side are the Japanese audience, but the English and the Danish crowds at either end are somewhere between the two. We are, with our chanting, our humour, our shouted warnings to the protagonists, our constant commentary on the action and our prominence when the action below us has been decided, a chorus.

We exit easily from the Big Swan by the lake. With no subway between us and the main station we can walk back to the city. It takes half an hour, but in the euphoria we hardly seem to notice the distance down the dark and tree-lined lakeside lanes. There are none of the lines of police guarding our way we had in Saitama to stop us drifting off route, just the occasional policewoman at a junction to show us the way. I wonder vaguely if it would have been the same if we had lost. And I can imagine even now the lights of the prefectural government office still burning as the officials ring their contacts in Illinois to find out what steps they should take with England fans after they have won.

Along the lane there is a love hotel, a place where space and sex-starved couples go to rent rooms by the hour. It is called something like Goodnight Vienna and on any other day would be the most secluded love hotel in town. But not today. As we pass it, a middle-aged Japanese couple are walking against the flow towards it, their self-consciousness among the English apparent in the stiff speed of their gait.

'*Ganbate yo!*' Rob says to the man. This single verb, which is translated sometimes as 'Endure!' 'Do your Best!' 'Work hard!' and even the objectless 'Challenge!' is used as an encouragement whenever there is some physical or mental obstacle to be got over. The word might not be translatable, but the man's reaction was universally male.

He was torn between showing his companionship with the woman, who had quickened her pace to get through the gate quickly in her determination to ignore this embarrassment, and his desire to acknowledge to Rob and us that, yes, I have just pulled. His expression pauses between the two and then resolves itself into a fake smile with a real twinkling in his eye.

We leave the lanes and come onto the main road where buses filled with England fans pass us by every second. It isn't Saitama, but it isn't Sapporo either. The locals are not lining up to congratulate us. A few housewives and restaurant grannies come out in front of their buildings to wave. A bus with the England band on it passes by, and it is like a scene from an advert. Crammed with English and thumping with the oomph and oompah sound of dented brass, it seems to sway with energy.

We have to go through the station to get to the main part of town. The Danish flag, an off-centre white cross on a red background, looks like a shattered and colour-reversed version of the cross of St George that is hanging next to it. It looks like it has been shot by a Dalek, which is probably how it feels.

We walk down through the alleys near to the station, past a bar that proudly proclaims 'NO TV NO BEER' and start our celebrations in the gaijin bar Immigrants, but it is strangely quiet. Just a few English and a few game Danish singing 'We *are* going home'.

Ken and Gemma are going home too. Their tickets and their time have run out.

'It's better this way,' says Ken. 'At least we are going home while England are still in.'

They go back to the station, and for a moment I think of going to see what is going on there, the streets of Niigata being so quiet. Instead, however, I go on to the Black Pig, but it is the same there. The police have cautioned the owner to keep his customers off the street in front of the pub or face being shut down. So he has employed an Australian bouncer to keep everyone either inside or well away.

It is between eleven and twelve on a Saturday night in June, and I am in the centre of a city of half a million people which has just hosted the biggest event of its history, and there is no one on the streets. The recession could never have been this total, it is impossible not to draw the conclusion that the Niigatans are scared.

I realise I haven't eaten and with Rob and his mates having broken away, I go into a traditional snack restaurant near the Black Pig. Unfortunately they do not have the usual picture menu, and suddenly the paucity of my Japanese is exposed. There are only two things I can think of to order: *sashimi*, light delicate slithers of raw fish, and *furai chikin* – knobbly over-chewy bits of deep-fried chicken dripping with fat. It is a culinary combination that I top off with sake and consequently an almost certain sickness.

I am on my own, but I will not be for long. If you sit there they will come, and they do.

'Where from?' says a lad in a Japan shirt who is kneeling at the next table along with two girls.

'England.'

'Ah Beckham, Owen . . .'

I have had this conversation perhaps a hundred times now, but it is only a ritual exchange, a sort of pre-chat bow, and anyway this lad is better than that.

He thinks hard. '. . . Rio!' he says, one I have not heard before.

'Yes, yes, Rio Ferdinand.'

Over the next 20 minutes or so we chat between tables. They are three students studying pharmacology, medicine and disorders of the blood at the university, but none of them are from Niigata. They are all 20. Then I ask for three more sake glasses and a fresh clay bottle and offer them a drink.

We talk about the soccer generation in Japan, and the English.

'We hope to be different, but our parents . . .' begins Miyuki, who has trendy square glasses. But her mobile phone keeps going off and taking her away from the table.

'When we were young baseball was most popular,' says Koshin, the lad, 'but now it is football. I want to go to England to watch Premiership.'

'In traditional role girls pour sake,' says Miyuki when she returns. Akiko, the other girl with longer hair, politely refills my clay cup.

'English people talk weather, family talk and weather talk, we think,' says Akiko.

'Football is one ball,' says Miyuki. 'If we get one ball, football will be world sport. A few Japanese will help the Afghanistan people to send soccer ball and uniforms and socks and shoes. So they help the Afghanistan people to play soccer.'

KICKING

139

'In Japan England is popular,' says Akiko.

'Not just Beckham,' adds Koshin. 'Arsenal and Manchester United, the Toyota cup.'

'I met tattooed supporter in McDonald's,' confides Koshin. 'I was a little afraid. We heard hooligan can't come to Japan. Japanese policemen is strong defence, too hard, too careful.'

'Did you speak to him?'

'No. Do you think there are hooligans in Japan?'

'Yes, but not so many.'

'*Eee.*' They sound surprised.

There is only one place to go in Niigata that night which is not dead: the gaijin-organised warehouse party down by the river. There are less English there than there were Irish two weeks before, but it is just as packed as it had been with young Niigatans. Again the atmosphere is what anyone would hope for from a World Cup, but not without English ribaldry. One English lad is teaching two Japanese girls a chant that I have not heard before, 'We take it up the arse. We take it up the arse.' This is a form of cultural fusion which might surprise the girls if it was ever explained, or demonstrated. But there is a more straightforward session of cultural fusion happening in a dark tranced-up room at the back. A group called Dan has developed an ultra-modern approach to traditional Japanese instruments. It's a three-person *samisen* group backed up by drums. The samisen is the three-stringed Japanese guitar which is the source of the irritating twang that accompanies Japanese *kabuki* and *No* dramas, but they are playing it at a break-wrist speed which gives the sound something of the energy of drum and bass. One of the men is older and has obviously broken away and in very Japanese arrangement has collected two acolytes to form his own samisen school – drum and twang.

But even though this event is the best thing I have yet seen in Japan, I begin to think that for the first time I have missed the party. It wasn't in Niigata, I realise. It was on the trains on the track back to Tokyo. They must have become one long conga of English celebration, because there were hardly any of us left in Niigata. So, even though it is near one in the morning, I head back to the station to see.

Hundreds of volunteers, railway staff and police line the concourses and platforms. I walk up through an aisle of farewell formed by their bodies. As I get up towards the tracks I am handed a gift pack which contains some sort of can of drink, a packet of biscuits and some leaflets about Niigata. The leaflets are either in Japanese or contain redundant information about the arrangements for the game and I find hundreds of them dumped near the bins on the platform. A shinkansen is ready to leave, one of the dozens of extra trains which have been laid on to ferry the fans back to the capital. The authorities were obviously counting on Tokyo's capacity to once more fragment the crowd and absorb any potential problems caused by the presence of thousands of English fans. But there won't be any problems. On the train the happiest and most replete England supporters ever seen dance in the aisles or settle into their seats to enjoy their beer.

I open the drink and cautiously take a sip. It is a cold milk-less and undrinkable oriental tea. Three lads on the shinkansen are watching me to see my reaction. 'Bleugh!' they mouth and parody throwing up. It is all grins and thumbs up and thumbs down. Any vestige of English coldness towards unknown compatriots has gone. 'What about the biscuits?' I ask in sign language. They nod, and gesture that in comparison with the drink the biscuits are OK. They are called Food Calorie Mate Sticks and are lollipop-stick-sized dry crunchy near-tasteless somethings. 'Each stick at ten calories', it promises. The lads wave as the shinkansen pulls out. And the last thing they see of Niigata is the station staff waving and holding a banner which reads 'See You Again'. It is 1 a.m. and the JR staff will carry this on for at least another hour, but the sense of relief in that banner and in the posture of the police and the guards is obvious. We have hosted England, we haven't had any trouble, and they've left. Thank God.

KICKING

TOKYO

Japan 0 Turkey 1
16–21 June

I BROUGHT *MOCHI* BACK FROM NIIGATA FOR THE KAWAMES. I had to bring something but I had no idea what I was buying. It turned out to be mochi, a sweet gluey beaten rice product that is as unpalatable as its description.

'*We must have this with green tea, very tasty,*' said Mr Kawame. 'Thank you very much.'

This gift was *omiyage*, a present brought back from travelling. All the towns in Japan have edible delicacies associated with them and this one came from Niigata. It is rather like bringing back Cumberland sausages from Cumberland, but organised in a peculiarly Japanese way. I could have bought this Niigatan glue-delicacy in a shop in Niigata, in Niigata station, on the shinkansen from Niigata to Tokyo, or in Tokyo station where there are shops catering to people who want to give the impression they have taken the trouble to buy a gift while travelling through Japan. But buying it in Niigata station felt more authentic than buying it in Tokyo, and it was also the only way I could be sure that I was buying Niigatan omiyage.

'*This is Niigata omiyage?*' I asked the stallholder at the station.

'*Yes?*'

'*What is it?*'

She told me at length, but all I was able to catch was the last few words, '*. . . do you understand?*'

'*Yes, delicious.*'

And they did turn out to be the most delicious mochi I had ever eaten, which is not saying much as all the mochi I had ever eaten until

KICKING

143

then I had done so while performing an etiquette calculation. How much of this stuff do I have to eat? All of it? And if not all of it what is the minimum amount I can get away with? Is it better just to try it and then say it's delicious, but that beating rice to mush is considered wrong in our country, or should I try just a little more and then pretend I'm full, but, it's only a baby-sick-sized portion anyway, no one's going to believe it would fill up a huge gaijin like me. But what if I'm actually sick? What would be worse, just trying it or eating it all and risking throwing up?

This was stream of consciousness about streams of vomit that passed through my mind when contemplating mochi.

But the expensive mochi gift I had brought back from Niigata was actually edible, and, as all gifts are in Japan, very well presented.

There were at least four different layers of wrapping, through plastic to paper to wood, but the final wrapping was of bright-green leaves that looked like they had been plucked off the stem that morning. It was like peeling back the layers of civilisation.

'Very natural,' said Mr Kawame approvingly.

Underneath each of the five leaf-wraps was the turd-sized offering of mochi itself. The outside was a dull-green-coloured layer tasting of green tea while the centre was a mud-coloured layer tasting of mud.

Sophisticated dining in Japan involves a complete lack of sophistication. They eat with twigs, kneel on straw, and wrap their sweetmeats in leaves. As in the tea ceremony, all the sophistication is contained in the manipulation of these simple elements in an aesthetically pleasing manner. Getting a block of very sticky rice mush out of the foliage it came in and into your mouth is not easy to do with style. Somehow 16-year-old Tatsuya was unwrapping his like a choc-ice leaving the mochi standing just proud enough to take a bite. You could actually see how the green outer layer and brown inner layer had retained their integrity. Mine was different, brown and green layers quickly merged into one another as the goo clung to every surface it came into contact with. It was like a training film for forensics. Mochi got under my fingernails, on the table, under the table and into my ears. At one point I was reduced to sticking whole leaves into my mouth and scraping off the mochi with my teeth.

Having successfully brought back some omiyage, I try to entertain the Kawames with the tales of my travels.

'In Sapporo, big party, thousands of young Japanese and English fan on the streets, drinking, dancing, singing, until six in the morning.'

'Impressive.'

'Then I went to Sendai and saw Poets' Islands, then Osaka, very many police. Then Niigata.'

'That's a very tough schedule,' says Mr K.

'In Niigata I went to the court.'

'Oh dear.'

'An English fan to a Japanese ticket having sold person was arrested.'

I find the lawyer's handout, which is in Japanese on one side and English on the other, and show it to Mr K. He reads it through, explains it to Mrs K, but does not really say anything.

'In England only two days for arrest,' I say. 'In Japan twenty-one days, for English people very long.'

But I am not condemning my hosts' country to them, only comparing.

'I think it's a good thing,' says Mrs K, quite sharply.

Mrs K works as some sort of police clerk so what she said was not perhaps unexpected. What was unexpected was that she reacted at all. Most law-abiding Japanese tend to assume that if you have got yourself involved with the police then you are likely to be a criminal, and so try to have as little to do with the police as possible. Mr K's non-reaction was, therefore, much more typical. It may have been motivated by the realisation that this sticky subject would only cause controversy between us and would be better left alone to avoid disturbing the harmony of his household and our relationship. It may have been that just talking about the police was too close for comfort. Or he may have realised that, having heard me describe John Jones as a 'to a Japanese ticket having sold person', the chances of us having a meaningful discussion about the relative merits of British and Japanese jurisprudence were going to be severely constrained by my lack of language.

For the next three days we are able to watch the rest of the last 16 matches. Obviously I have no idea whether the Ks would have watched quite so many games if I hadn't been there. Mr K and Tatsuya seem to be interested and both have some knowledge about the game; Mrs K is interested in that it is a new experience for her; and 13-year-old Asuka isn't interested at all. I am sure they would have watched some of them, but every evening they kindly put the telly on just as we are sitting down to supper, and together we sit through six hours of dull football.

'You have come here for the World Cup so we should watch it,' says Mr K, perhaps also giving himself permission to watch the football during dinner.

So, over the next few days we watch the Irish lose to the Spanish, the Brazilians beat the Belgians, and the Koreans beat the Italians. Fortunately for Asuka, all but three of the eight second-round matches finish in normal time, and only one of them, the Irish game, goes to penalties. This however is the one point where we all become equally interested in seeing what happens, and even Asuka put aside her homework to watch. Football purists have always argued that penalty shootouts aren't football, that the game would be better if it always finished in normal time, and the authorities always seem to be talking about new ways to avoid the necessity of a penalty shootout. Judging by the reaction of the Kawames this is probably a mistake. There is no greater reward to the unaligned and uncommitted football viewer than getting to see a penalty shootout after a dull drawn game. There is universal human drama in watching exhausted and stressed footballers under a weight of pressure from the expectations of their nation, their fellow players, and from themselves, fail to do the one simple thing for which decades of training, preternatural athletic gifts, and vast rewards in wealth and glory should have prepared them: putting a ball into a goal from a distance of ten yards. It may be a humiliation that football purists would like to avoid, but a penalty shootout undoubtedly increases interest.

Unfortunately it is only the Irish who manage to bring all the Kawames together. But they provide a penalty shootout of such spectacular incompetence and indignity that it holds the interest of a 13-year-old Japanese girl who knows nothing about the game.

Watching football on Japanese telly is an ego-boosting experience. Having watched thousands of hours more football than the Ks I am transformed into a man with a profound knowledge of the game. While they react to the play, I am ahead of it. In fact I am even ahead of the commentators, whose contribution to the event is to say *'chance'* or *'here's a chance'* or *'that was a chance'* when the ball approaches, enters or leaves the two end-thirds of the pitch. This serves to alert their listeners who may be treating football as if it was baseball or sumo: sports in which quick bursts of action are preceded and followed by longueurs. Japanese telly also has a habit of exaggerating the importance of the score at the end of the first half as if football was a game of two innings. At one of the England matches, Sapporo I think, the score on the stadium noticeboard was presented as two separate totals: First Half 1–0; Second Half 0–0; with the total added up underneath, just like a baseball score. Helpfully, however, all the technical language has stayed in Japanese-accented English: *yero cardo, goalu, offusido, hando* [-ball], *corna kicku*, although they use *PK* to mean penalty kick. Also, instead of saying last-sixteen, quarter-final and semi-final they say best-sixteen, best-eight, and best-four, which, when we fail to progress to the best four, begins to sound tauntingly inaccurate, given that it includes Turkey, South Korea and a Germany we have beaten 5–1 at home.

Tatsuya and I amuse ourselves by pencilling in the results of the upcoming games. Obviously Japan will beat Turkey and then Senegal, while England's victory over Brazil will lead to a Japan v. England semi-final. Traitorously, yet politely, Tatsuya concedes that England might win this, leaving England to play Germany in the final. Like many Japanese football fans, Tatsuya had a favourite foreign team, and his team is Germany. Trying to explain to him in basic English why it is that the English and the Germans don't get on in World-Cup-world is beyond the subtlety of my Japanese so I make do with the brutally blunt but fundamentally accurate observation that '*English people hate German football team.*' Despite this, and even more traitorously, he won't concede that Germany will lose to England in the final thus making him more a supporter of Germany than he is of Japan. We are so convinced of this scenario that we even make up some scores. However, our ability to predict the result of football matches purely on the basis of what would make us happy is about to be exposed.

I have five days before the England game and, although I do spend a couple of them sightseeing, I feel, in a Zen-like way, that I am getting more out of simply being (at the Kawames). It's also a lot less effort than going to another highly ranked group of pretty islands because at the Ks I can gain most of my cultural knowledge through the television.

KICKING

147

The Ks don't watch that much telly, but they have it on in the morning during breakfast and it reminds me of nothing so much as local telly in the UK. The news from beyond Japan is sketchy, while the news from inside Japan tends to be dominated by three themes: little-people criminality, big-people corruption and what the plants and animals are doing this month. Little-people criminality is just the everyday sex and cash crimes you hear about all over the world. Big-people corruption is, however, more typically Japanese in that it involves the fall from grace of either a politician or a company president due to bribery.

Like many cultures that extend gift-giving beyond family and friends, it is sometimes difficult for the Japanese to tell the difference between a gift and a bribe. And, of course, bribery and corruption stick together like mochi and green leaves. Spotting the difference between a gift and a bribe isn't as hard for Westerners. If the gift in question is not mochi but a large amount of cash donated by a construction company to a politician who is about to make a decision about a construction project, then most Westerners will tend to opt to define it as a bribe. Japanese politicians, however, live in a culture of gift-giving and it seems to be very difficult for them to spot that the bales of yen being delivered to their office might be motivated by anything more than the ritualised kindness of an acquaintance. Unfortunately, many Japanese politicians get caught in this sticky lexical trap. They usually rise to prominence on a platform of reform and fighting corruption, then someone tips off the press to the fact that this platform is held up by piles of cash donated by the construction industry, for example. They are then pulled down into the mire, with ten-thousand-yen notes sticking to everyone they know. Finally the politician retires to become a power behind the throne of the next wannabe reformer. The fate of their politicians thus has at least a metaphorical and probably a direct link to the fate of the whole Japanese economy.

But what really typifies the Japanese news is the proportion of airtime given over to the doings of plants and animals. Sometimes they are even the lead item, and the best example I ever saw came from the early 1990s.

With the right equipment certain programmes on Japanese telly can be listened to in English. This allows you to hear, for example, the original soundtrack of an English-language film, and the same facility can be used to listen to a live simultaneous translation of the national broadcaster's main six o'clock news. For the interpreter, who is usually American, this is a high-skill, high-stress job, and, although there are occasional and unintentionally hilarious mistakes, they tend to do a good job. It is very rare that the interpreter makes so many mistakes that the information becomes unintelligible. But one day something very odd happened. The lead story on the national six o'clock news was about a kingfisher. There were lots of shots of the bird flying into its riverbank nest to feed its young. This wasn't the odd thing. I was quite used to valuable minutes of the main national news being taken up with stories about flora or fauna. This was about the time that the Eastern bloc was collapsing and when Gorbachev was losing control of Russia so there weren't really any big stories to cover.

But the interpreter kept making mistakes and, as this wasn't really a hard news story, I couldn't understand why, particularly as the mistakes were at a level of grammar that even I wouldn't have made. He kept using 'I' instead of 'she'.

'And the female bird is returning to her nest with food for her young,' he said. 'I am, no she is very happy to be able to provide food for her growing brood. It makes me, er the female bird, quite excited to fish for my, no, her young. There you are, my children. Er no, the female bird is providing . . .'

It took longer than it should have to work out what was going on. But it dawned. He was using the wrong pronouns because the female newsreader was acting the part of the mother bird, and was cooing her pleasure at providing her food for her young. At this stage in the history of female emancipation in Japan, the female newsreader's primary role was to look at the male newsreader and say *'Really?'* in a variety of inflexions. Occasionally she would also be allowed to add an adjective. *'Complicated isn't it?'* she would say, glancing at her male companion for a reassuring restatement of the story, which at length he would then give her. Of course the female presenters were allowed to read the softer news items, but articulating the feelings of an anthropomorphised female kingfisher must have been a highlight in this woman's career.

But, apart from a story about strawberries ripening in Hokkaido, which isn't anthropomorphised, as *'How excited it makes me to turn slowly red'* is a humiliation that even the Japanese wouldn't put their female journalists through, I don't see anything as poignant as the kingfisher story. In fact the female newsreaders now seem to be taking an equal role to the men. There are women reporting on the sport, and one who, every morning, reports from Japan Railways in Tokyo on any problems with the trains. Given the perfection of the rail transport system, this is as redundant a role as sending a journalist down to the Thames barrier to report daily on any problems with the tides in the hope that she might one day get a Canute scoop.

During the day, the telly moves to soap operas and talk shows where six or seven bright young things sit around talking about the issues of the day in front of a non-participating audience: a sort of Japanese version of Richard and Judy, Richard and Judy, Richard and Judy. As the World Cup is on, a lot of their discussions revolve around the strange behaviour of foreigners. Sometimes they do pieces on England fans. One item shows an England supporter failing to eat *onigiri*, which is a something-wrapped-in-rice-wrapped-in-seaweed snack. The England supporter does not understand he has to wrap the separately packaged dry seaweed round the sticky rice before he can begin. He launches into the rice and produces a similar effect to the one I achieved with the mochi. This provokes laughter. To maintain cultural balance, they then show some Brummies eating crisp sandwiches. There is also a discussion about the lack of hooliganism, and they show a shot of gangs of photographers looking depressed after Sapporo because they have had no hooligans to film. The programme even plays sad music over the images of their dejected faces to emphasise the point. The bad behaviour of the home supporters is also discussed, and there are shots of broken umbrellas and fast-food wrapping piled up in the gutter after one of Japan's matches. The reporter interviews a street cleaner and asks him what he thinks about the mess the fans have selfishly made.

'*They're not really football fans,*' he says, or at least I hope he does because it would have been nice to hear the phrase that is always used of hooligans being used of Japanese fans who had merely been careless with their litter. But he may have said '*It's not just football fans [who leave litter].*'

Obviously I cannot get all my culture from the telly, mainly because I can't understand most of it. But I can go to the net. This is the thing that has changed the experience of being in Japan most since I was here. It is claimed that the net brings people together, but this is only true of individuals. Ten years ago my girlfriend and I had a long-distance relationship that my parents and even my grandparents would recognise. We wrote each other letters which took a week to arrive and which crossed each other inconveniently on the way. When we spoke on the phone, it was brief because of the expense, and stilted because of the delay on the line. We were also cut off from the context of each other's lives. The only news I could get of the UK was from a short-wave radio that was sometimes so thick with static I could not hear it, and from airmail newspapers that were a week old. All that has changed. Staying in touch is easier, but being closer to the UK, being able to e-mail and read about what is happening at home has the strange effect of taking me further away from Japan. I have no need any more to struggle with what I hear on the telly, or force myself to see what tiny fragments of knowledge I can gather from newspapers. It also makes Japan seem stranger because I can never cut off from Britain. The first time I was here I had slowly become used to the alien conventions of Japanese media culture until they became nearly normal to me. This couldn't happen anymore, because everyday when I go on the net I am reminded of how different they really are.

So in search of Japanese reality one day I go to Tokyo's Ueno Park to see the museums. Ueno Park is a rare area of green in the middle of Tokyo. Its vistas provide a horizontal rest for the eye from Tokyo's ubiquitous vertices and its tree-sheltered benches provide homes to hundreds of derelicts (who take their shoes off when they go to sleep). There are dozens of separate school parties in the park. They have come from outside Tokyo for a cultural visit to the capital. But the presence of the derelicts does not seem to worry the teachers or their charges who gambol unaccompanied through the woods without worry. As I pass through, some of the derelicts are queuing for food handouts, and seemingly without any intervention from the charity workers they form themselves into blocks which are as precisely ordered as any drill-ground platoon. The very neatness of the rows contrasts with their shabby clothes and thinness, and makes the whole scene sinister, as if they were broken-spirited refugees from their own country.

A large matron in a flowery dress, 60-something and eager, comes up to me while I approach the museums.

'What country?'

'England.'

She grabs my hand and shakes it too loosely and for far too long.

'Your football team very strong. I would like to congratulate your Queen on her 50 years.'

She has obviously been looking for an England fan to say this to for some time, and it was kind of her to say it. But I could think of nothing to say in reply.

'Thank you, thank you, that's very kind. Goodbye.'

At Tokyo National Museum at the end of the park the Japanese predilection for ranking is once more on display. The Museum contains 91 items which have reached the level of National Treasures (that is the highest, or Thora Hird level), and 616 objects which are ranked as Important Cultural Properties (a sort of Kenneth Branagh level) with another 100,000 also-rans.

Many of these 100,000 items appear to be pots. And although there are enough swords and armour to keep the little boy in me happy, it is the pottery that dominates. The Japanese are very proud of this pottery because the people who lived in Japan 10,000 years ago were the first in the world to start making it. The world's first pots are conical in shape so cannot stand up on their own, and despite the reputation of the modern Japanese for rapid innovation it took their ancestors several thousand years to work out that it would be more useful if they made their pots with a flat base. The pots are still in use, however, but these days they are used to tell the story of Japan. This is presented as waves of influence, primarily on pottery, as first Korean- and Chinese-inspired or imported pots begin to appear. They are followed by Central-Asian-influenced designs and even, towards the end of the first Christian millennium, pots with a distinctly Greco-Roman look. Finally in the last section there are Turkish-looking designs and Delft on display.

All this is very different to British history. Tokyo Museum suggests that only pots and not people ever came to Japan, and that the Japanese stayed the same but were merely influenced by other cultures. In contrast, British history presents itself as a series of waves of assimilation in which Roman-Celtic Christians, pagan Anglo-Saxons and Vikings, Norman overlords and other waves of émigrés and immigrants were absorbed into the country, none of them being able to claim they were more authentically British than anyone else.

I walk across to another of the museum's buildings, the Horyuji Homotsukan which houses the 319 Horyuji treasures given to the imperial family by a Buddhist temple. Here there are enough Buddhist statuettes to try the patience of Buddha himself, but it is the building in which they are housed that seems to me, despite its modernity, more authentically Japanese than anything it contains.

It is approached across a flat bridge of grey slabs, which that day are blackened by drizzle, and between two shallow rectangular pools of water. There is no one around and for a moment I think it is closed. I walk across the wet and shiny bridge between the pools and it feels as though I am walking on water. There is no one in the entrance hall to disturb the sight lines or the silence, and immediately the proportions of the building begin to work on me like music. Though I have dried my feet, they leave ghost prints on the grey granite slabs of the floor. My footprints fade even as I watch.

I am so thrilled by this building that I go outside and play through the whole of my arrival again, just as if I am repeating a piece of music. This time jets of water burst through the surface tension and fill the forecourt with the sound of falling water. It is only in the silence afterwards that I become aware of the water dripping from the trees.

The building was designed by Yoshio Tanaguchi and is in three layers. The roof and curtain walls are a continuous inverted U-shaped curve providing protection to the glass box of the interior proper, which itself contains a stone-walled central enclosure in which the Buddhist relics are housed. The counterpoint between the light of the entrance hall and the darkness of the central chambers, between the heaviness of the rock and the airiness of the glass, and the overall harmony of the building's proportions creates an aesthetic experience which is as profound as any produced by music. And in its subtle control of my movements as I approach, its concern with proportion, its revealing changes between sound and silence, and in the transitions between interior and exterior, it is very Japanese.

The odd thing is that when I go out onto the terrace for coffee I forget for the first and only time that I am in Japan and speak to the waiter in English. It is the best coffee break I have ever had. I sit under metal awnings, watch the fountain spurt, hear the drizzle on the trees, and see where the rain has curved in under the awning to create organic curves on the rectangular slabs of grey. Everything is perfect in its simplicity, all modernist marble and metal, a simple cup and saucer, ashtrays I want to nick. The only jarring note is the teaspoon. It is too heavy and ostentatious in its pretence that it is made of silver. Seeing it against all this simplicity, makes me, in that one moment, understand how in the tea ceremony every detail must be correct to produce the aesthetic effect. In this way the architect and the managers of the hotel chain that runs the coffee shop have provided me with an insight that saves me from ever having to be interested in another tea ceremony again.

On Tuesday I go into Tokyo's nightlife and skyscraper centre, Shinjuku, to see how the Japanese supporters will behave after their second-round game against Turkey.

'Be careful,' says Mr K, 'dangerous.'

The game is being played in Sendai, but Shinjuku was where two telephone boxes had been smashed up after Japan's first World Cup victory in Yokohama, and, according to the newspapers, it was where a crowd of Japanese supporters had surrounded and taunted a group of riot police who had found themselves cut off from their colleagues. It also has a big open-air public screen outside the station so it should have been a natural focal point for Japanese fans. Stupidly, however, I had forgotten that there is nowhere in Japan where you can watch the games in the open air.

If one of the defining images of this World Cup for television viewers was the tens of thousands of Koreans gathering in parks and plazas to watch the games, for those in Japan the defining experience was wandering through the streets asking whether you would ever find anywhere that was showing the games.

This is my problem that day and I wander up and down the drizzly streets of Shinjuku looking at first for a convivial bar or coffee shop in which I can watch the game, and then just for anywhere that is showing it. I am in the techno-heart of Tokyo, the place that inspired the cityscapes of *Blade Runner*, where everyone seems to be in constant gadgeted contact with everyone else, but I cannot find anywhere to watch the national team playing a football match in one of the country's major cities.

The open-air screen is on, but it is showing adverts and a message which says unapologetically, 'It is Not broadcasting any watch for 2002 FIFA World Cup.'

Eventually I find a branch of Wendy's hamburger restaurants which has a telly next to the counter on the ground floor. It is packed with damp and desperate Japanese fans, and judging by the groans that are coming down the stairs there is also a screen on the first floor. Once again I cannot see the score from where I am squatting but I reckon they must be 1–0 down with the final whistle fast approaching. It is a temporary thing, this telly, and it has been positioned with its wires stretched to taunting point. At one point it flicks off and the crowd moans. A handsome Wendy waiter comes out from behind the counter and gives the thing an untechnological slap. The telly sparks back up. We all clap and he bows low with some nice big-city boy irony, but it's the only clapping we hear until the end of the match. There is a gaijin sat behind me. We are the only two in the restaurant and I'm sure he is American. But we do the Tokyo thing and ignore each other. The final whistle is greeted with silence and another long groan. It is the gaijin behind me who starts the clapping. Perhaps the Japanese did not know what to do in defeat, as they had not known what to do in victory. Perhaps they did and they wanted more empty silence to better contrast with the clapping, but it is the gaijin behind me who starts it, and everyone joins in.

Out on the street everyone knows Japan has lost and the drizzle seems to put more disappointment to the air. Young men in blue greet each other with '*Gokuro sama deshita*', which means something like 'we tried hard', and even hug each other in the stiff bear hugs that they must have learned from the English. Cars pass honking their horns; people are hanging out of the windows with their clapping machines flailing.

Under the big 'Not broadcasting any watch' screen, a crowd begins to gather and chant and sing despite the rain. Once more they are all under 25, but things have changed since Sendai two weeks before. There they had only been able to chant '*Nippon! Nippon!*' but the Tokyoites have learned some more tunes. '*Arigato Nippon*', they sing and '*Nippon Saiko* [Japan is best]'. They have obviously been influenced by the behaviour of foreign, possibly English, supporters because they now have Japanese words for the tune to 'Go West' (or '1–0 to the In-ger-land'). They even do-do-do-do-do-do-doo along to *The Great Escape* accompanied by brass and drum in certain imitation of the English. There is irony in this. It is the theme to a film about British prisoners attempting to escape Germany during the last war, the screenplay of which was written by James Clavell who had been a prisoner of war in a Japanese camp and who later went on to write *Shogun*, the book that more than any other introduced Japanese culture to the West. Then they sing 'Kimigayo', the Japanese national anthem, the first time I have heard it. Their resistance to singing it must have been broken by the realisation that without it they are going to have an embarrassing paucity of songs, or perhaps its mournful tune better suits defeat than it does victory. There is even someone wrapped in the imperial flag in which the rising sun is more than just a dot, but spreads its rays across the white background in a way that almost everyone else in South-east Asia finds frightening. But he wasn't emblematic. There are also supporters clothed in superhero costumes, some with golden Buddha masks, and another in white face paint and a white wig who has painted his nose into a red dot so he looks to me like a clown.

There are lots of police here, however, obviously determined not to allow any more telephone boxes to be destroyed. But like their colleagues in Sendai they do not bother to pretend they are traffic cops. In the centre of the square beneath the plasma screen are two small raised areas of trees surrounded by low walls. The police are determined to stop any potential leader from occupying this higher ground and so line themselves up on the wall in front of the fans. A big lad with a trumpet wants to stand on the wall but is dissuaded by a policeman. Then one man in a full-body transparent rain mac, which doesn't scream tough-guy in any culture, tries to leap up on to the wall but slips, or is shoved roughly backwards by a policeman. Immediately five or six police grab hold of him. There is no attempt to hassle him quickly out of the way as I have seen with the English. Instead a mobile stand-off takes place. The police and the fan stare each other out and veer across the square first one way and then the other, as if he was the tumbler at the centre of a ouija board. Then a decision is made and he is taken away. He may not see anyone he knows again for three weeks.

This was Japan's last *banzai*, but it went the way of the banzai in Sendai and fizzled out in the drizzle, although here there was no attempt by the police to disperse the crowd. This was Tokyo; there would always be more young people coming out of the subway to keep the numbers up and any attempt to disperse them would have been both confrontational and, in Tokyo's endless series of city centres, pointless. But despite these differences between the two cities, both times that I had seen post-match crowds of Japanese supporters the same thing had happened. The crowd had gathered, started to celebrate or condole, and then, long before anything criminal had occurred, been stopped. Nobody knew what was going to happen. The fans had never supported a successful Japanese team in a World Cup, let alone one in their own country, so they did not know what would happen. The police had never had to deal with this type of crowd for the same reason so they didn't know either. It was obvious that this generation of Japanese was trying to use football to find its feet, but it was equally obvious that the police had no intention of letting this happen.

The same night, in a cruel quirk of the scheduling, South Korea play Italy in their last-16 match. Japan and Korea have a similar relationship to England and Ireland: repression by the former, an understandable sense of grievance from the latter. But they are yoked together by geographical proximity, common traditions, shared culture, immigration, and, in Japan and South Korea's case, another cruel trick by FIFA in getting them to co-host the World Cup. England and Japan are also similar in that both want their neighbours to do well, but only as long as they don't do as well as England or Japan. There was already a sense that Korea had made more of an impression on the world than the Japanese because of the enthusiasm of their vast crowds of supporters, but now there is the possibility that Korea might advance to the quarter-finals.

I get back to the Kawames in time for the second half, and Tatsuya is getting angry with Korea's refusal to lose.

'Nice keep,' he says every time the Italian goalkeeper touches the ball.

'I think Korean fans are more desperate to win than the Japanese,' says Mr K sniffily.

But they do win and Tatsuya is sulky for the rest of the evening.

Despite this natural adolescent reaction to South Korea's victory, the Kawame household is a domestic idyll. In fact, even to draw attention to Tatsuya's slight disgruntlement is too much. Neither he nor his sister is ever anything but impeccably behaved. Even the difficulties of being teenagers seem minor compared to Westerners.

'Noisy,' Mr K would say of Tatsuya disapprovingly, but he wasn't really.

He and his sister would do their homework diligently and without prompting, and, because he was watching the World Cup, Tatsuya would sometimes stay up until past one in the morning completing an assignment.

He would be up again before seven the next day, like everyone else except me. Mr K would have to shout '*good morning*' through the sliding doors to wake me, and then we would all have breakfast together squeezed into the spaces round their circular dining table watching the breakfast news.

Mr K would always butter the inch-thick slice of toast that Mrs K had made and hand it to me so I could add jam or marmalade to it. This was a detail I never understood and which bothered me for far longer than it should have. Once I asked him why he did it.

'*It's because my wife is very busy in the morning so doesn't have time to do it herself*,' he explained.

But I never managed to ask why Mrs K would have done it for me in the first place.

They would all be out by quarter to eight and wouldn't be together again until nine at night. Mr K worked as an architectural consultant in the city and was always the last back. All the time I was there he made no attempt to disprove the idea that Japanese people work like the devil. One day he went to work as usual at seven-thirty and didn't get back until midday, midday the following day, having been out to work for 36 hours. Mrs K was the same. She worked in a police office near Saitama stadium and it took her two hours to get there in the morning and two to get back at night. One of the reasons I had come to the Kawames originally was the promise that it was close to Saitama stadium. I thought it would make a good base for the first England game and for the semi-final, both of which were to be played at the stadium. But by the time I had worked out that it was two hours away it was too late to change my arrangements. For me, the idea of taking two trips of that distance over three weeks had been enough to make me question the idea of staying with them. Mrs K made the same trip, there and back, five days a week. I have no idea when she got up, but she left the house at 7.20 and got back at the same time in the evening having commuted for half a Western working day.

In the evening Asuka would often get back from junior high school between four and five, but then she would usually be off to ballet or some other club and not return until between six and seven. We were often in the house together alone: an adult male stranger and a pre-adolescent girl but it never seemed to occur to the Ks, as it would to Western parents, that there was anything odd about this arrangement. Next Mrs K would come back, then Tatsuya around eight, and Mr K around nine. Every time anyone came in the house they would say '*Tadaima*' (I'm back) and the answer '*Okaerinasai*' (Welcome back) would come without fail. If either went unheard they would be repeated until both had been said, or it had been established that there was no one in the house. It was like an English family's 'good morning' or 'goodnight', an incanted phrase to mark the transition from one state of being to another, but in Japan a phrase was also needed as you cross the threshold from outside to inside as well as between sleep and wakefulness.

At seven we would have something like tea: Japanese green tea with crackly salty snacks or some cake. We never ate the main evening meal until Mr K had returned, which meant we would often not start until after nine. It was very late but like breakfast it kept the family together.

This was another of the myths about Japan that the Kawames were disproving. I had heard that Japanese husbands rarely spent any time with their family because of their workload and that the wives therefore ran something similar to a single-parent family into which the husband came like an unwelcome intruder.

One of my Japanese teaching colleagues had once appeared to provide evidence for this hearsay. We had finished work early and we were driving back towards Niigata when he asked what we should do.

'Why don't we just go home early?'

'I can't go home.'

'Why not?'

He looked embarrassed.

'I don't have a key.'

I knew him quite well so his embarrassment didn't bother me, and I suspected that his lack of a key had something to do with his wife not giving him one.

'What do you mean you don't have a key? I don't understand this aspect of Japanese culture, could you explain?'

'My wife will be out and I don't have a key.'

'You don't have a key to your own house?'

'Of course I have a key,' he said touchily, 'I just do not usually bring it to work with me because my wife is always in when I get home.'

'In England we say that every Englishman's home is his castle, but in Japan . . .'

'Hmm.'

So instead of going home early we went to a coffee shop to wait for the time that his wife would get home.

Mr K, however, had both a key and a relationship with his family. After the dinner that had been delayed for his arrival, we would talk about the day, the children would practise the piano, Tatsuya and I might play chess, and Mrs K and Asuka would do the laundry. Asuka did it happily, but Tatsuya had to be prompted and did it sloppily.

'*Women's work,*' he said.

When the football wasn't on, there were sometimes big budget samurai dramas to be watched. In these all the women coo like doves and all the men talk as if their lungs have been replaced by internal combustion engines and their voice boxes by exhaust pipes which have had a hole punched through them by a dodgy car dealer to achieve the correct level of grating groan to the actors' voices. At the end of the show, and this is something you only see in comedy shows in the West, one of the actors in full samurai dress might encourage us to watch next week and give a précis of the action.

Later, everyone would take showers in succession. Japanese bathrooms are the same size as those in the West but the entire room is waterproofed. For a shower you stand by the side of the bath and wash yourself on the tiled floor. There is usually a mirror at knee height and a stool to squat on for shaving. Bathrooms are arranged this way because the Japanese all use the same bath water, and therefore everyone washes before they get into the bath. But no one took baths at the Kawames in the two weeks I spent with them so the arrangement was another relic of tradition.

'*Excuse me for going before you,*' Mr K or Tatsuya would say to me before using the shower.

This didn't refer to any problem with the hot water supply, but to the tradition that the guest should use the bath first when it was hottest and cleanest.

The only negativity to this idyll of domesticity was the negative of all idylls of domesticity: it edged, with all this piano practice and game playing, towards the dull and the worthy. I never heard music coming from either of the kids' rooms, although they could have used headphones when they went to bed, and Tatsuya did once play a computer game. But there was no separation of teenager from adult. Everyone was always unfailingly polite. Mrs K would cheerfully box her son's ears, but there were no harsh words and no withdrawal from the family space. It was no wonder then that for young people only a little older than Tatsuya the boisterous, authority baiting and belligerent English should have been so fascinating.

The Ks taught me a lot about the Japanese. While I was there I realised that for all my having lived in Japan before I had never once stayed the night with a Japanese family. The most important thing I learned was to stop bowing quite so much. As a foreigner in Japan the more you bow the more you feel like you are doing the right thing, and it took me a long time to understand that bowing at every opportunity made me look ridiculous. It was as if I was a Japanese guest who shook the hand of his English host at inappropriate times: in the morning, after being handed a cup of tea, when they left for work, when they took a shower. After a while I stopped, and the Ks were probably grateful that they no longer had a nodding dog of a gaijin bowing at them at every opportunity.

Japan was starting to un-get me.

TOKYO – SHIZUOKA

England 1 Brazil 2
21–26 June

'I'M ON THE TRAIN WITH TWO ENGLISH HOOLIGANS.'

The American ticket tout is talking on his mobile phone.

'I've got what you wanted and I'll meet you at the station. Bye.'

'Don't judge people by the way they look,' says the Englishman to him when he closes his phone.

The Englishman is short but strong and wiry with close-cropped hair and the sort of lined, sun-aged face that puts him anywhere between 30 and 50. There was no menace to what he had said, it was just a statement.

But the ticket tout had not been judging either of us by our appearance. He just knew he was with two Englishmen and so had wryly referred to us as hooligans.

The three of us, the ticket tout, the sun-aged Englishman and me, are standing together in the narrow connecting corridor of the shinkansen to Shizuoka. The train is packed with Japanese travelling between Tokyo and Osaka, and with English and Brazilian supporters on their way to the match that afternoon. There are no spare seats, no reason to move, and little way of getting past the pack of people in the corridors and in the aisles.

The train is throbbing with anticipation. Only five English people had witnessed the circumstances of John Jones' incarceration, and, of the many thousands who had passed through Niigata, very few of them would have realised how lacklustre the city's welcome had been. The vast majority of English are still in their deep-heat love of this event, and they had hurried through Tokyo station en route to

Shizuoka like they were on their way to a much-anticipated wedding.

Everything before today was teasing prelude. Sweden, Nigeria and Denmark did not have our self-defined status in World-Cup-world, and any loss to them would have been humiliating. Argentina had to be beaten. But today, for the first time, we are playing a team that is worthy of us: the only team in the world that it would be acceptable to lose to. We are going to see the first meeting between Brazil and England in a World Cup since 1970 when they beat Alf Ramsey's World Cup-winning team. If we win, we will be the first people to have witnessed an England qualification for a World Cup semi-final for 12 years and only the third generation ever to do so. Unlike the uncertainty before Saitama, the apprehension before Sapporo, the air of dull necessity around Osaka and the confidence before Niigata, the atmosphere before this match is one of unsuppressed excitement and thrill.

The excitement entwines itself around us and despite our differences the three of us – the ticket tout, the sun-aged Englishman and me – make a good fist of getting on, and, anyway, the sun-man needs something the tout should be able to supply.

'Have you got me a ticket yet?' the sun-man asks after the tout has another phone conversation with a contact.

'Hey, I'm working on it, I'm working on it.'

He has a lazy manner, this American. It may be an affectation designed to defuse the antipathy felt for him by his customers, but it makes him easy to get along with.

'I should have snapped up that ticket I was offered on the plane,' says the sun-man, turning to me. He had flown in from London that morning, on a whim, all the way to Japan for England v. Brazil. And although he was a football supporter this was the first England game he had ever tried to see.

'This bloke said he had a spare and said he'd sell it to me. I don't know why but he didn't want to give me it on the plane. We said we'd meet in baggage claim and I hung about but he never turned up. Maybe he thought twice about doing business with someone who looked like me.'

'I had a deal lined up yesterday too,' says the tout, 'with the Saudis, for final tickets. I met them in a hotel but they were asking double face value. They were just being greedy, one of the richest associations in the game, and they were being greedy. It would have been sweet though. I don't mind it so much with the Africans, but with the Arabs . . .'

'What's your mark-up then?' asks the sun-man.

'Sixty per cent, 70, 80 per cent, it all depends.'

'On what you can get away with?'

'On lots of factors.'

'How much would you charge me?'

'That depends on how much I paid.'

'Look, give me your number and then at least I can get hold of you if I can't get a ticket.'

The sun-man takes out his mobile phone.

'I can't get it to work,' he says.

'They don't work here,' I say.

'It works in America.'

'Yeah,' says the tout, 'but it's a completely different system here.'

'So how have you got one?' I ask. 'I thought you needed a Japanese address.'

'They did act up in the shop, but I told them "Look, do you want the money or don't you?" and they wanted the money.'

The tout gives the sun-man his number, and the sun-man enters it into his useless mobile phone.

'So where do you get your tickets from? Is it always off the national associations?'

'Yeah, look.'

The tout takes an envelope from his waist bag and cautiously pulls three quarter-final tickets halfway out, keeping them at hip height. He points to the place where the holder's name is printed. The top one has JAWOC on it, Japan's World Cup organising committee.

'How did you get into this then?'

The tout tells us. He started selling tickets to gigs in his hometown and it kind of built up from there. Now he has a partner and a legal business: legal in some states but not in others. They also organise tours, in this case for the South Americans living in the US who wanted to come out and support the old countries.

'It's more of a grey area here, though,' he says.

'It's not a grey area,' I say, 'it's illegal.'

The tout just smiles apologetically.

His story prompts the sun-man to tell his own. He too had worked the edges of the music business, promoting his own band at festivals in France and further abroad. Then marriage, and when the kids and the bills came along he became a builder in London. He tells stories about corruption and intimidation in the building trade and how cocaine has become almost an alternative currency in the capital, and we talk about Millwall and the club's efforts to curb the violence there.

'It's not my club,' he says, 'but they are trying.'

Then, with the kids grown up, a change. He had begun an as yet incomplete media studies course and the change had contributed to the breakdown of his marriage. After the divorce he sold the house so he now has the freedom and the money to come to England v. Brazil on a whim. But this is no laddish thank-God freedom. He has found it difficult learning to communicate with people again without a companion to talk things through with, and he finds it hard with the women.

It is impossible not to like this sun-man. He is open and honest, and his appearance, contrary to his own impression of himself, is not intimidating.

'I wish I'd got that ticket on the plane,' he says again.

'There'll be a ticket,' I reassure him. 'I haven't been to a game where I haven't been offered one.'

Japanese people squeeze past us on their way to or from the toilet, or on and off the train. At some point we pass Mount Fuji. I have never seen Fuji in the iconic flesh, and, for a tourist's simple sight-collecting reason, I want to. But each time I have passed it on the shinkansen something has prevented it, cloud, sleep, or conversation, and, on this occasion, the train is too packed even to glimpse it through the window. But it lies near Shizuoka stadium, and seeing it is the one inconsequential thing I want to do while I am there.

We try to stay close to the tout when we get off at Shizuoka, but a single customer, even a single customer with whom he has established conviviality, is not enough to keep him close. He slips away through the crowd, and, as we are waiting for the local train to the stadium, we see him for the last time. He surfaces on an adjacent empty platform looking for the contact he cannot find.

'What should I do with this?' the sun-man asks, holding up the smoking stub of his cigarette. 'I'd chuck it on the track but everywhere's so clean.'

He has been in Japan just a few hours and already it has got him. We go up to the smoking area and he puts it in the ashtray.

'I don't even know your name,' he says. 'I'm Mick, but you guessed that already.'

So he is Mick the builder from London.

But it does not look good for Mick. At the exit of the station nearest to the stadium is a long corridor. It is lined with beggars: Japanese, English, Brazilian. They hold up signs trying to convince us of the genuineness of their need. They speak to everyone who passes, 'Spare ticket? Spare ticket? Spare ticket?' Their presence creates in me the same useless pity that beggars do everywhere, and the same horror. Because, but for a quirk of the ticket-allocating system, I could have swapped places with any of them, and because I know that this is my last ticket and, should England beat Brazil, I will be in their place in a few days' time.

Football fans have a horror of touts, and the beggars are there because they want to find the mythic spare ticket, the one that has become spare by accident, the same spare ticket that the lawyer Takashima said John Jones had found himself with after his friend had been 'over-drinking'. According to the fans, a spare ticket should always be sold at, or very close to, its face value.

'If I had a spare ticket, I would sell it at face value.' Almost everyone says this, though an avaricious few will add for themselves a small profit.

Some of the reason for this is pragmatic. The ticket has an American-dollar value printed on it, so unlike other goods the purchaser is always aware exactly how much profit the seller is making. Taking too much profit would be a social and, in the mêlée of a football crowd, a physical risk, because the purchaser would never forget your face, and never forgive your mercantilism. Of course the fan with a spare ticket could always sell it to a tout, but the touts are probably aware of this difficulty and exploit it.

But the main reason that fans do not sell their spare tickets for profit is democratic. They do not believe the allocation of this pass into World-Cup-world should be determined by the ability to pay. Entry should be obtained either through luck, that is, through FIFA's Internet draw, or through the commitment schemes operated by the official supporters' organisations. It is like citizenship; it should not be sold.

But of course it can be sold, and the fact that many of the sellers are corrupt insiders only throws the fans' idealism into relief. The touts are loathed for the same reason. They bring only mercantile values to the transaction. For them, market forces set the price of the ticket, and their profits reflect their risks. In Japan, they are trading illegally so their risk is made double. Not only might they be arrested, they also go unprotected from the actions of opportunist thieves and the yakuza.

But the fans' despisal of the touts is more profound than a mere lack of appreciation of the risks the touts are running on their behalf. To them the touts and the corrupt officials who supply them are like medieval pardoners selling easy entry to the kingdom of heaven.

This conflict between the market value of the ticket and its immeasurable value to the fan is also embodied in the ticket itself. Like other fans I keep it safe in a money belt that also contains large denomination notes and my passport. The ticket seems to take on the attributes of both. With its dollar value, security hologram, serial number, transferability, swirling design and tendency to inflate, it seems like money. But with its named bearer, its visa-like concern with time, its function to allow entry into a place, it is also like a passport into World-Cup-world.

There were more ticket-seekers at this match than at any of the previous four, and Mick's desperation increases when he realises how great is the unmet demand. As we pass down the station corridor we start our own muttered requests to everyone we pass, 'Spare ticket? Any spare tickets?' and everyone we ask responds either with a sad shake of the head or a 'sorry'.

In front of the station there is a large rough-gravel forecourt surrounded by dozens of temporary World Cup stalls. There are wooded hills all around, and in the hot mid-afternoon sun it feels as if we have stepped out of the urban modernity of the Japanese train system and into a country fair. But for one thing, there are too many people. There are thousands packed into the corral of the wide circle formed by the stalls.

Immediately we are in the open air Mick gets a lead. A long-haired English lad responds with something other than 'sorry'.

'This Japanese bloke's got two going spare. One's mine, but . . .'

In the moment it has taken to tell Mick this, the Japanese man has disappeared.

'Where's he gone? He was here a moment ago. He's got my ticket. And my money.'

We all scan the milling crowd, but there are Japanese men everywhere and only the long-haired lad knows who we are looking for.

'There he is.'

Twenty yards away there is someone who is obviously circling us through the crowd. He looks suspicious and he watches us suspiciously. We are standing at the entrance to the station and there are policemen all around us. The ticket seller had been spooked and had retreated into the relative safety of the crowd.

Mick and the long-haired man go over to him. There is some nodding from the Japanese and then a shaking of his head. I watch the policemen watching this for a moment and then I go over.

'He'll sell it to me,' says Mick, 'but I've only got pounds. He won't take pounds.'

'There might be somewhere you can change some money,' I say. 'I'll go and find out.'

I had done this myself at Niigata, but there you could only change fifty thousand yen (three hundred pounds) and I think Mick will need more. But I go to the information kiosk anyway.

'Is there anywhere you can change money?'

The five patient, OK-English-speaking women in there hate themselves for having to say no, but in the end they have to.

'We think no,' they say.

I start back towards Mick and the ticket seller. But a minute or two after I have left the information kiosk one of the women runs up to me.

'Please, there is a machine to change money.'

In her eagerness to help she has left her kiosk to search among the thousands of English gaijin for me. But she isn't any help; I am sure she means an ATM, and I feel a mix of gratitude and irritation at her eagerness to help and her incapacity to do so.

Mick may feel the same about me, because when I get back the ticket is gone.

We walk over the rough gravel following the curve of stalls. One of them is offering a telescopic view of Mount Fuji. I pause and think about going over, but we are too busy asking the illegal shirt and pin sellers who have set up pitch in the circle of stalls if they have any tickets.

A tout comes past us, whispering on the move, 'Do you want a ticket?'

He moves through the crowd like desire personified.

'How much?'

'A thousand pounds.'

Mick is indignant.

'Pounds?' I ask stupidly, knowing even as I say it that touts do not mistake dollars for pounds. He is five yards away, but he bothers to turn his head and look at me with as much contempt as if I had asked him if he meant a thousand yen.

We are nearing the end of the stalls. Beyond, where the path begins to go up the valley towards the stadium, there will be no more chances. Then a final lead, a lad who must be on a pact with his mates. He has two tickets but he needs another three and if he can't get them he will sell those he already has.

Mick wants to stay with him and I want to go up to the match so we part company. I tell him about Paddy Foley's pub in Tokyo's Roppongi, that a lot of England fans might end up around there, and we wish each other luck.

So I leave the circle of stalls with their touts and money-changing, overpriced official merchandise and cheap black-market merchandise, and immediately the atmosphere is calmer. The path winds up through the hills, over bridges and past woods towards the stadium that sits like a temple on the top of the hill. It is the most spectacular approach of any of the stadiums we have been to, and a combination of the late afternoon heat, the long country walk, the flocking crowds and this coliseum in the distance makes it feel Roman, as if the city has come to the country for the games. The excited shouts of tens of thousands of people start as a murmur in the distance and, as I get closer, build in the air like the tension before a storm. It is impossible not to quicken as I hear it, and with the rest of the crowd around me, my pace and my heart speed up.

This is what defines sport, this quality of liveness. If football allows us to see what people are like by limiting their actions and their goals, and restricting the time and space in which they can achieve them, it is their freedom within these limits, their freedom to show us what they are made of, and their freedom to determine our emotions for us that makes it so exciting. When we leave this stadium in two hours' time we will either be experiencing a profound depression, or a euphoria that no one English has experienced for over 30 years. And we do not know which. There is no spectacle on earth like it.

It is the opposite of art. Sport is live; art is replay. The first prescribes actions; the other pre-scripts them. To show us the human, films, books and plays put no restrictions on the protagonists' time, space, or action. But in return the protagonists have no freedom. They always do and say the same thing. This is the attraction of art. You can experience the emotion an artwork creates as many times as you want, and with each repetition your time is repaid as the emotion deepens in intensity and gains in complexity. It is a trick that even works over thousands of years and across cultures.

Sport does not do this. The further away a sports event is in time the less it reverberates. Rewatching a match only gives the viewer a fraction of the original emotion. There is none of the compound interest that art generates. But the intensity of sport's liveness is its own reward. The anticipation on the walk up to the stadium is unlike anything that art can provide; the terror and hope it creates is beyond the contrivance of the predetermined endings of narrative art; the joy and pride, despair or dishonour experienced when the outcome is decided is more personally felt in a football crowd than it is in any other audience.

For the first time I have no one to share this with. I know no one in the stadium. Ken and Gemma have gone home. Rob may be here somewhere but his plans were vague. The lad who hugged me is nowhere I can see, there is no one I even recognise from previous matches. But it does not matter. The enormity of this game so overwhelms my individual circumstances that I do not need some connection within the crowd to anchor me to it.

Once more we listen to the opposition sing their national anthem in silence. Once more some of us add 'No surrender' to ours, but it is fewer and fewer at each match. Down below me are three men who are dressed in something that is neither a Far Eastern addition nor a retreat towards the image of the gentleman. All three, one white and two Asian, are wearing white turbans with the cross of St George painted on the front. These two icons, Islamic and Christian, seem as far apart as the distance between the hooligan and the gentleman, but they have managed to meet in the strange contradictory brew that is the English. They look nervous, these three men, as if they have not done this before, as if they are concerned for how that section of the crowd that will not tolerate cultural compromise may react. Or perhaps they have already worn them and had some reaction but are determined not to be intimidated.

Midway through the first half we score. The sun is shining low in the sky; there are trees just visible on the hills surrounding the stadium. We are at an event that everyone had said would not work, but which has worked better than any World Cup that the English have been to before. And we are 1–0 ahead of Brazil in the quarter-final of the World Cup. It never gets any better to be English in Japan.

'It's like watching Brazil,' someone at the far right of the England end shouts, and there is laughter, and the chant gets taken up in a wave through the crowd, the only wave the English will do.

Then the crowd begins to sing 'We Shall not be Moved', the first time I have heard it in Japan: a song of religion and protest, but not a well-known song. The words at the song's centre are fluffed, something about a water-line, and as if in ridicule the Brazilians score.

At the start of the second half and for the first time in my life I am watching football to the same level that England are playing it. Brazil get a free-kick far outside the penalty box and it does not occur to any of us, the fans or the players, that they could score from there. I am watching the box, waiting for the cross, and suddenly, without intervention from any of the players clustered in the penalty area, the ball is in the net. The Brazilians are cheering, their players are running about in delirium. The English, players and fans, are stunned and struck dumb. It is a moment of horror, as when a vampire rises and hovers in mid-air. Everything we know about what is possible in a football game is contravened. This isn't Maradona's Faustian theft of a skill from the real world. The physical laws of the real world have been broken in a way which to the Brazilians is miraculous and to the English is terrifying. It is not possible for the ball to have taken that trajectory from such a distance. Even the evidence of the replay on the large screens at either end does nothing to reconcile what we are seeing with what we know is possible. We crane round to look at the screen above our heads. We need to see it again and again before we will accept that the impossible has happened. After the match we still cannot accept it. 'It was a fluke,' people say. 'He meant to cross it.' We would far rather believe that this evil miracle was some kind of fluke helped by a disturbance in the blustery warm air than accept that one of the greatest players from the greatest footballing country in the world meant to score a goal.

A little later Ronaldinho is sent off, but we never find out why. It happens far away, as his goal did, at the other end of the ground. Although they showed the goal, the big replay-screen now fades to black. Then it shows the score. But we know the score, we know we are losing 2–1 to Brazil.

'What happened? Why don't they fucking show it?' someone asks.

This has happened before, every time anything controversial happened at the previous games the screen would fade to black. But this time it feels different. It feels like Soviet-style censorship in FIFA's meta-state. Seven thousand miles and eight hours away in the free world, we know that the whole of England will know what has happened. This has rankled before, but we had never been losing before. Until Brazil's second goal, World-Cup-world had seemed a happy place, but now everything becomes the object of our frustration.

The Brazilians, now they are in front, begin to waste time. The referee does nothing about it, and we hate him for it. He is the man in black, the forbidding lawyer, policeman and priest, and though there is a natural antipathy towards him because he intervenes in the free play of the beautiful game, his failure to uphold the rules makes him despised.

The Brazilians and the officials are the focus for our frustration but they are not its source. It is obvious that England are never going to score. There is never an attack that ends near the Brazilian goal, and, as the final minutes flick away, even the England players begin to fall like foreigners in the penalty box in a way that does not make us proud.

The shouts of 'England' fade; 'The Great Escape' sounds hollow. There is no belief, but we adopt the posture of fervent belief. We stand, our hands to our mouths or to our faces, wishing . . . but the whistle blows. There is not enough time added on, but there would never have been enough time. We were never going to score.

The leaving of the stadium is a quiet, profound affair. No one hums 'The Great Escape'. No one sings with English humour, 'We're all going home', or 'We only sing when we're winning'. No one sings anything. Even the Brazilians are quiet. There is nothing but quiet chat among the groups. The sun is setting, the wind is cooling. At the bottom of the valley the shinkansen passes through in silver streaks of horizontal lightning. We are a river of people flowing sluggishly down the valley. From above, this forlorn streak of white mixed with yellow looks like something from an epic film, a migration through the green and pleasant land. We are leaving the Promised Land and the walk back down the wooded valley feels like the exodus it really is. We pass over the bridge slowly. Far below us, too far to jump in heady celebration, only in despair, a few England fans who had somehow escaped the lines skip across the grass. They are happy but only because they are getting to the station quicker. But it is nice not to be alone, it is nice still to be in the crowd. It seems to hold the moment together, even though it is dispersing into the memories of all of us. In an instant we have ceased to be citizens of this fantastic world of national heroes and now we are just tourists who have somehow fetched up in Japan. At every other game we had been to we left making plans to go on to the next event, but now we are talking of going home. Immediately the conversation turns to plane tickets, and rumours are repeated about there being no flights out of Japan until 8 July, some three weeks away.

The first people from the real world we encounter as we near the station are a line of five or six Frenchmen.

'They're here to taunt us, the bastards,' says someone.

But they don't, they don't need to, although they look pleased.

We go beneath the shinkansen tracks and as the bullet train passes above us it whistles, but it is not the whistle of a signal, it is just from the displacement of air around the train. Beyond, at the station entrance, the Brazilians are waiting to catcall. There are about a dozen of them, joined by a few Japanese in yellow shirts.

'Bye, bye,' shout the Brazilians waving in cruel delight.

There are no big knots of English to create a confrontation, but whenever the Brazilians see any small group of us their chants get louder. A line of police is stringing a rope between the shuffling humiliated queue and the taunting Brazilians. One tall man, his face dark and with long black hair flying, replays the goal, hitting an imaginary stationary ball with the side of his foot, stubbing it, the very lackadaisical quality of the shot adding to our humiliation. He hits it with the side of his foot, like a lazy dad playing with his toddler son. What can you do but hold your head up and walk on by? Though when one catches my eye and opens his lips to taunt me I look away.

I have no idea what it was like to be Brazilian at that moment. For me the fantasy that our best 11 men could take on the world had ended. England failed. We also ran. And though we were beaten by the eventual winners, there was no comfort in knowing that we were just taking our place in a memorial list of the vanquished: Turkey, China, Costa Rica, Belgium, England, Turkey (again) and Germany. I have no idea what it can be like to believe in the fantasy of football success so fully that it rises out of the unconscious to become an event in the real world.

They are waiting again in the low-roofed concourse of the shinkansen station. But here there are English who are prepared to look them in the eye and take them on.

Two heavy men, with thrusting torsos and pointing fingers, stand firm in front of the taunting Brazilians and shout 'Fuck off.'

A Brazilian woman, not one of the bikini beauties the television laps up, but someone who is shorter and stubbier and tougher bustles chin up towards them and screams a stream of Portuguese in their direction.

Behind her a man is chanting with desperate conviction but no fear, 'No fight, soccer. No fight, soccer.'

But there are police everywhere and the English stomp off seething up to the platform.

On the shinkansen I sit next to a man who works in insurance and holds a season ticket to Chelsea, though it is only home games now. He is perhaps 38, too old to bother trundling around the country, and his knees have gone. He sees me light up and comes to use the ashtray in the armrest next to me. We chat for a while, but he looks so uncomfortable I offer him my seat. Eventually the Japanese woman in the next seat, who has been staring out of the window into the dark such is her nervousness of the English, gets off. I go to sit beside him and we spend the journey chatting about Japan. But I am tired of hearing about how wonderful the Japanese are, of how he thought they would be shy, of what a revelation it was to him that they are not, of how in this bar there were just the two of them and the owner brought out a telly and they tried the oddest food . . .

My mind, like everyone else's, is turning back to home.

But when I get back to Tokyo about nine that evening I go to Roppongi one last time. Our loss has altered everything. As I pass through the packed streets even the shouts of 'Beckham, Beckham' sound taunting and ironic.

In McDonald's, at the counter, an Englishman betrays his irritation as the Japanese manager counts out in English numbers the eight hamburgers he has ordered for his mates.

'Oh, your English is so good,' he says loudly and sarcastically, aping the empty compliments of the Japanese.

Above in the seating area, three Chinese men in England shirts talk about the future price of the dollar.

'Everything has changed,' says a young Englishman eating alone. 'Everything has been taken away from it. I was loving it, but all I want to do now is go home.'

The steps above Paddy Foley's, where three weeks before the Irish choir had ignored the police request to 'BE QUIET', are roped off to prevent further displays of exuberance. While below, in the urban cavern in front of the pub itself, dozens of English are making plans.

'Thailand for me,' says a Geordie. 'I've still got two weeks' holiday so I am going to use it.'

An old Japanese man dressed as a cowboy holds up a sign saying 'Let me draw your face'. One of the group the Geordie is with takes him up on his offer. As he caricatures the Englishman, he caricatures his artistic self by sizing the Englishman up with his pencil, held horizontally then vertically. Then he turns his sign around. On the reverse it says 'Do you want to hear my song?' His sitter and the group say no, but he hits the button on his tape recorder anyway and 'Begin the Beguine' starts to play. A tramp, drunk and bearded, holds up his fist and exhorts the salarymen to fight the English.

Then I see Mick.

'You brought me bad luck,' he grins.

After I had left him, the police had followed him around and given him no chance of finding a ticket. He had watched the match crouched by a portable telly owned by a Brazilian who hadn't even watched it but who spent the whole of the game calling the English wankers.

He chats up a couple of Japanese girls, but has no luck with them either.

'They liked you,' I say.

'I thought so.'

'It's difficult to tell with Japanese girls.'

'I thought they liked me.'

'What went wrong?'

'They said they had to go and I asked if I could go back with them to their hotel room.'

'What did they say?'

'They laughed and they said yes. Then they left.'

A woman detaches herself from the two men she is with and with chutzpah and charm because she knows from our tops that we are English says to Mick, 'I am German.'

'She's not German, she's Polish,' says one of the men. They are fat and 40 burghermen from anywhere, mid-European to mid-Atlantic.

'Maybe she learned it after the occupation,' says the other burgher laughing. 'It's German with a Polish accent.'

But their snide sniggers show they know they've lost this girl.

She is a Germanic blonde in Germanic denim, and she likes Mick. Soon they are leaning into each other like a slow-mo Status Quo dance.

I leave him to it. As I walk back to my hotel, the sound of 'Vindaloo' is drifting down from a bar along the road. On the pavement the prostitutes are clustered. The madams pinch me in my side as if feeling a slave for fat. *'Masagi? Masagi?'* the girls ask, and for a moment I think they are going to manhandle me into their parlour such is their desire for fat English wallets. It hadn't been so blatant three weeks before, but it is a Friday night and perhaps they realise that the biggest concentration of foreigners, the English, are about to leave.

I go back to my hotel, but a couple of hours later am woken by the sound of sirens and go out to see what is happening. Although Paddy Foley's is shut, there are still a lot of English down there. The restaurant next door is selling cans of beer from a tub of water. The English are singing their English songs, gathering themselves for the next tournament. Two men in cream jackets and cream shorts are standing on the wall using long flexible batons to conduct the crowd below them in the pit. Brazilians come and go along the street. They are chanting, the English chant back. A couple of black Americans stand laughing on the steps and chant 'USA, USA,' to be met by sing-song taunts of 'Who are you? Who are you?' The wand-wavers in cream go to take on the Brazilian chanters, and a policeman directing traffic tries half-heartedly to take their batons away. The police are relaxed now, they have seen it all before, they think they can control it. It is all amicable.

Then a German lad turns up. He cannot be more than 17, all red hair and happy youth, like the boy Becker. There are a few more Germans, an older man in his 20s among them. It is the middle of the night and nearly everyone is drunk. Slowly the Germans move to the top of the steps.

'Deutschland, Deutschland,' they chant.

The English at the top of the steps and the men in cream shorts and jackets react.

'Two World Wars and One World Cup. *Funf ein* to the In-ger-land. *Funf ein* to the In-ger-land,' they shout, waving their batons at the Germans.

It is all good-natured taunting. The cream-dressed men think that they control the powerful hatreds of real-world nationalism and use them just for play.

'Two World Wars and One World Cup.'

The Beckerboy has a German flag. He waves it, and the English down below begin to realise that their enemy has occupied the high ground, an enemy that has qualified for the semi-final. The friendly baiting of 5–1 goes on above but the change in the atmosphere comes from those below. The English who don't want trouble have instinctively moved away leaving just a hardcore of perhaps ten to face the four or five Germans. They don't like the fact the Germans have the high ground. One stands down below in the semi-darkness of the pit, his arms wide, his big chest and bigger belly jutting out proud, shouting 'England, England'. He looks like a fat Buddha hung on a cross, a triptych of images: Christ, Buddha and John Bull. Another climbs the steps, big and burly, he is singing 'Rule Britannia', but the competition is no longer just about volume. Though he is singing it is just prelude. He advances, and the Germans and their Japanese hangers-on retreat, not in a moment of confrontation but in a quiet realisation that there is more here than they wish to handle. The 20-something German has disappeared. The English singer, his objective achieved, turns and marches back down the steps. He pauses and then tenses his muscles and raises his arm in a fascist salute: a triumphant taunting of his enemy's darkest hour.

An amateur cameraman on a bicycle is circling happily around the pavement recording everything. The Japanese neutrals who have been sitting on the steps watching all of this never move. Unlike the other English and the older German, they never sensed that this was a situation that could have got out of control.

But the boy Becker and his mates stay where they are at the top of the steps. They are puzzled. They can sense that there is a problem, but they cannot understand it. Another Englishman, his torso naked, three lions tattooed onto his chest where the badge would be if he had been wearing an England shirt, sees their puzzlement and takes it upon himself to explain. He tells Beckerboy he is too young. He says it with concern and his meaning is clear: you are too young for me to fight, but be careful, you do not know what you are doing.

He is right, and wrong. The boy does not know that taunting these Englishmen is a mistake. The other, the older one, who isn't too young to fight, realised this so has quietly moved away. But the Becker boy has worked out the flaw in the Englishman's argument, for if he is too young to be fought what pressure is there on him to move? And in his youthful ignorance of human nature he stays and shouts 'Deutschland' a few more times. The Englishman does nothing. The moment passes. None of the English step out of the chorus and become protagonists. Instead they go off with the Americans to find a nightclub.

'No fight, soccer. No fight, soccer,' said the Brazilians.

It is only a game, not worth fighting for. But that is its peculiarity. It is only a game. Unlike other games, the individualism of chess, the interconnectedness of Go, the martial masculinity of sumo, the machine-like masculinity of American football and baseball, the earthy masculinity of rugby, the gentlemanly conduct of cricket, the Olympian ideals of track and field, football demands no identifiable qualities of its players apart from skill. It is just a game.

Even its origins in English villages are irrelevant: two messy teams of yokels attempting to move a ball by any means through fields and lanes between goals a mile apart. It has gone from this to the precise elegant glances of legs, feet, torso and head; the space restricted, the time limited, the match refereed, hands outlawed but for the lonely one left at the back. Only the ball and the goal remain. The ball is the subject, the goal the object. The ball goes in the goal. It is so simple. It is like a primer in English grammar, but it is not a primer in English culture. None of its roughneck origins remain, and it has never become the carrier for any cultural philosophy that could limit its appeal among the nations of the world. It is only a game. And it is this universal simplicity that makes it the perfect place to play with nationalism.

....

I had meant to stay until the end, but the attraction of watching the Germans and the Brazilians progress inevitably to World Cup glory while the English were forgotten did not make me want to stay. The only thing that might have kept me in Japan was the South Koreans winning their semi-final and coming in their tens of thousands to Tokyo for the final. That would have been a moment which, given their histories, neither country would ever forget. 'They'll lose the semi-final,' the Japanese joked nervously and nastily to themselves over the next few days, 'they won't want the expense of coming over to Japan.' I took a risk that the Koreans would lose and booked myself onto a plane that left Osaka the day after they played.

I spend the last few days at the Kawames and then travel from Tokyo to Osaka for the last time. Once more I fail to catch sight of Mount Fuji, though this time it is because I am sleeping.

There are not many people on the shinkansen, but even though I am bored with limited conversations about football and Beckham, I am glad I do not ignore the grey-haired and bearded man who sits across the aisle from me and who attracts my attention. We smile; he has a wonderfully open smile, filled with good humour.

'What country?'

'England.'

'Ah the England football team is very strong. But they do not always win. Luck, isn't it?'

He has lived in Tokyo then Osaka but now is living in Kyoto, so he has moved backwards through Japanese history as if his life were a capital collecting game. I ask him about the difference between Osaka and Tokyo. I tell him that I think the girls in Osaka are more sophisticated and cooler. But he just nods and smiles, as if the difference between the girls of one city and another is not the most important question in the world to him. Instead I talk about the trains and how bad they are in England compared to Japan, and of the recent crashes.

'I am surprised at that,' he says. 'England was Japan's teacher in many things. I would believe it in India or China, but not in England. It isn't mentioned in the papers.'

But there is not a lot of talk about trains, and we move on to roads where at least the congestion is something to complain about in Japan. He laughs. He laughs a lot.

'I drive a car. My friends are very surprised at this. Is it safe they ask. My father always said cars were not safe.'

I cannot make him out at all. He looks about 50 but he does not have the work-blitzed blankness and lack of range of the salaryman. I look at his longish grey beard, and assume, because the only Japanese I have ever met who had beards were bohemians, that he must be an artist.

'Excuse me,' I say. 'How old are you?'

He laughs because of my bluntness so early in the conversation.

'Can you guess?'

I say about 50, but now I know I must be a long way wrong.

'Really? You make me very happy. I am 72.'

It is a rare thing to meet a Japanese old person alone. Usually I would just be introduced to them merely as a courtesy, as had happened at the Kawames. And all the hot soup of their children's hospitality kept conversation safely and domestically dull. I would see them on the buses and on the subway trains with their football-kit-wearing grandchildren, the old people showing their love by standing while the children sit down, and I would wonder at how vast the change had been from the nationalism and feudalism of their own childhoods. But coddled by their families and their children, and hampered by my lack of Japanese, I had never been able to talk to them about the past. But on this empty shinkansen, I have a conversation that was unlike any I had had before.

'When I was a child the roads were all mud and sand,' he says. 'The main roads were very good, in tarmac, but once you get off them it was mud and sand. There were horses with carts behind. We waited until the man had passed and run and jump on. It was our game. Also we had carts with oxen. Oxen, is that right – cows?'

'Oxen is right, but we don't have those in England, only a long time ago.'

'Ah yes,' he giggles, 'a long time ago.

'When I was ill the doctor came to our house in a rickshaw which he had employed. My mother twisted a coin into a piece of paper and gave it to the driver as a tip.'

'How old were you when the war ended?'

'Sixteen.'

'Were your parents very worried you would have to go into the army?'

'Yes, they were very worried. But when I was in the second year of junior high school we were sent to a fuel-processing plant in Kanagawa prefecture where we worked on rocket fuel.'

I am uncertain that he meant rocket fuel. I thought only the Germans had developed the technology at this stage, but I trust his word.

'It sounds very harsh for young boys but we were very happy because it meant no school. Then towards the end of the war food became very scarce. All we said was "We are hungry. We are hungry." All we ever talked about was food.'

He is laughing infectiously all the time as he is speaking. But whether from embarrassment at the subject, or his memories of his and his friend's humanity, or to avoid the pain, I do not know. Because I am not old and because I have never suffered.

'Once when the persimmon came into season we saw that the farmer had a great many of them on his trees. We drew straws for who would go and I was chosen. I went to the farmer to ask if he would sell the persimmons. He said yes and I took along a *furoshiki* [a cloth for wrapping things in] and filled it with persimmons. As I walked back to our dormitory I was very happy and proud. My companions saw me coming and stood in the windows shouting, "*Banzai! Banzai!*" But as I came close a teacher saw me and waved me towards him.'

He raises his hand and waves come-here in the Japanese style, his palm downwards and all his fingers wiggling, but then he remembers that Westerners do it differently and changes it to a palm-up gesture to help me understand.

'The teacher asked me what was in the furoshiki and I had to give it up. But sometimes the Navy people were very kind to us and gave us sweets and other things.'

'I have read that the Navy were less militaristic and nationalistic than the Army.'

'There are many opinions, and if I had the vocabulary in English I could explain better, but I cannot.

'Sometimes bad things happened. My friend was called Raisu. His family was very rich. They had a big garden and they built a big bomb shelter with concrete. Unfortunately, or perhaps fortunately, I do not know, my friend was visiting his family for his grandmother's funeral, and a bomb hit the shelter and they were all killed. If it had hit anywhere else, or they had been in the house, nothing would have happened.

'On the day the war ended, I walked back to my parents' home and I passed Raisu's house. It had a long wall and I looked inside. The house was gone, and everywhere was high with weeds. My family survived. Fate. After the war we counted the number of bombs that hit our relatively large garden. There were one hundred. Yet we all survived. Of course now they are all dead. But fate.'

I feel bad asking him about these memories for my own interest. So I ask about his grandchildren.

'She is one,' he says. 'I have one only. But she seems very stupid. I hope she does not become as stupid as me.'

He laughs. This is old-style Japanese courtesy, a belittling of oneself and one's relatives.

'Now nobody has gardens,' he says. 'I used to collect stones from the rivers to make into castles in our garden. I was scolded. But now the rivers are clean.'

I think he means they just run in concrete channels, and he looks out of the window to illustrate his point, but there are no rivers to be seen.

He doffs his hat and smiles and thanks me for the coffee I have bought him and says how sorry he is he has to leave. He is courteous

KICKING

183

and continues to doff his hat and bow slightly on the platform as he walks, sometimes backwards, away.

....

In any book about the English abroad it is essential to include something on foreign toilet manners, so the flight there and back was a tale of three toilets: Japanese, German and English.

In Japan defecation is just another act of humanity, and their toilets reflect this and even, it must be said, celebrate it. The Japanese have three levels of toilet: high-tech Western, mid-tech Japanese and simple hole-over-a-cesspit technology. The high-tech toilets are just Western toilets with a bidet and breeze function added on. A control panel next to the toilet roll allows the sitter to select the squirts of warm water and air he wishes to be aimed at his anus. This has often been used as evidence of how peculiar the Japanese are, but really this is only typically Japanese in that it is a space-saving device to preclude the necessity of having to house both toilet and bidet. The only thing to really concern the near illiterate Westerner is the fact that on the control panel the Japanese word-symbols for high- and low-pressured water-jets are 'like a horsefly' for high and 'with the strength of two bows' for low. It is difficult to know which to choose.

The very low-tech hole-over-a-cesspit is exactly as described, but the most common and therefore most typically Japanese is the mid-tech toilet. Superficially it has some similarities to Western toilets: white porcelain, a flush mechanism in silvered metal, a bowl shape. But this is where the similarity ends. The toilet looks like it has been designed by Dali. The bowl has been stretched and made shallower and dropped until it is like a small rectangle about a yard long that has been set into a low platform on the ground. You step up to the plate, drop your pants and squat over this trough (pull your trousers halfway down your thighs rather than to your ankles, as they will get in the way of the gravitational path between anus and earth). Apart from the position, what you never forget about Japanese toilets is the way that the faeces are consequently laid out for your examination. There they sit, not safely hidden in a funnel a foot below you covered in water as they are in England, but no more than an inch from the floor, uncovered in water, as if inviting you to probe them for smuggled contraband. Of course the English might not want to linger over this discovery, but this can be problematic the first time you use one. The flush mechanism is impossible to find because it is just a lever sticking out of the piping which does not advertise itself, and this in itself is internationally problematic as there are few people in the world who wish to ask for assistance in these circumstances.

In Munich they had been thoughtful enough and correct enough to include the apostrophe in the signs 'ladies' toilet' and 'men's toilet': a grammatical curiosity that has vanished in the UK. They were also sparkling; free of shit-splash and graffiti, everything was immaculate. But after a two-hour layover there was a sticker on the door saying Coventry FC.

Of course we have all done that at some time, had an urgent need to leave our mark, to squiggle on the dotted line, crayon the walls and disrupt the clean antiseptic lines of a Bauhaus shit-house. But you could tell you were abroad. Because the whole attitude to waste wasn't about dirt. Instead of the bins in the concourses being black shiny abysses of nothingness, each was a tricolour of coloured bags hanging from a hoop: one for each different type of waste. From above the trisected circle of the bin looked like a flag, a flag whose motto would be the efficient loving of the planet.

In England, if the toilets told a story, then waste, bodily waste and the bin-liner black hole, was a place where things were hidden rather than categorised and celebrated. They were also the home of the deeper horrors of the unconscious. At Heathrow, on the doors of one of the stalls someone had written 'BNP British Nigger Paki' and then below in possibly the same hand was added 'shit wanker'.

It wasn't only the toilets. After Japan, everything about England suddenly strikes you as different. As you fly in it is the division between the town and the country that you notice. There are neat ribbons of houses, snakes of terraces and semis. You see nothing like the jumbled, higgledy-piggledy alleys and neighbourhoods of Japan. In contrast it is the fields of England that are disorderedly organic; whereas in Japan they are such a grid of squares that you could give them postcodes. The light is kindlier and gentler; but the people are scruffier and less fashionable; it's more multicultural; the train seats don't recline; there are no helpful signs to tell you which railway carriages are reserved; but once you leave the towns it is all

KICKING

185

countryside; on British trains people talk to each other; although they are ruder; and it's dirtier. The underground trains shake like those in Tokyo would do only in an earthquake. Even the people who went to Japan are different.

One month before I had come from London via Frankfurt to Tokyo, and the plane had been full of nervy English, happy Irish and a few Germans. 'Go on! Get up! Get up you bugger!' the Irish had shouted as the plane took off, and I thought it might herald a 12-hour joke about an Englishman, an Irishman and a German on a plane, but it was very quiet. Only the Irish were in their colours, and though there were many English fans they thought discretion the better part of pallor, and kept their white kit in their bags. It was everyone's assumption that any display, of colours, drunkenness or chanting, might make them conspicuous and so in some chain of unreasonable events get them turned back from Japan, as we knew other fans had been. The nervousness increased as we waited in the queue for immigration. Nobody said anything, but all the English were thinking the same thing: that by some glitch in a database, a similarity of name to a listed hooligan, a similarity of face to a grainy picture of a thug, our inscrutably similar appearance to oriental eyes might combine to end our World Cup before it had begun. Only one man, a German, stood out, and his bravery defined the nervousness of the rest of us as we stood in the queue: a quick clappity-clap-clap 'Deutschland!' It was the first chant I heard in Japan and, from Beckerboy, it was also the last I heard.

The trip back reminded me of the nervousness we had all felt then, of the terror of the English that had swept Japan. But nothing bad had happened; it hadn't been John Bull in a china shop; instead, the Japanese had taken the English in.

'We're not as bad as they thought we'd be,' one English couple had said by way of explanation in Niigata. They were a young Asian man and his blonde girlfriend – Steve and Emma, professional – 'from Birmingham but without the accents'.

'They're surprised that we're not like they imagined,' they went on. 'We have a curiosity value. It's so repressed, this culture. It's all about respect. We're not. We're a lot more rebellious. I think England is more aspirational for them.'

'They love the way we thumb our noses at authority,' was one long-time resident's explanation, a head-hunter with his own business in Tokyo.

'So we're like manga characters, cartoons to them?' I had mused, and he had agreed.

In any book by a Westerner about Japan, there is always the temptation to come up with a grand unified theory about the Japanese: something that explains the complexities of one hundred million people in a few thousand words. So this will do as an explanation for why the Japanese took so to the English. We were like manga characters to them. We did all the things they were not allowed to do: danced, sang, chanted anarchically in the streets, and laughed at policemen. In Sendai and Shinjuku, the Japanese had tried to do the same, but had been stopped, and this made me think it was unlikely the World Cup would change the Japanese. What it had changed was the Japanese view of the English and, for those who went, the English view of the Japanese.

Long before the World Cup, England was seen as a gentleman country, but in one of the quickest and most complete reversals of a country's image ever known, England had become the home of the hooligan. The fact that nothing that could be described as hooliganism happened changed everything once more. There were many explanations for this. Some said it was due to the confiscation of passports and the issuing of advisory lists to the Japanese immigration authorities, so preventing some of those who might be expected to cause trouble from coming. Some said it was the intelligence of the policing. When they identified someone as a troublemaker the police went in fast and pulled people out quickly, giving no one time to react. They lined the streets, showed their presence, but never by their attitude invited or appeared to welcome confrontation. Some said that it was the organisation. Despite the lack of open-air screens and the unwelcoming over-regulation of the indoor viewing arenas, the care with which the needs of the fans had been attended to was admired, particularly the attention to travel arrangements. Others thought it was the victory over Argentina. A loss would have brought the Argentines into the centre of Sapporo to celebrate, but there were just too many English in the city that day for any of us to consider skulking in our hotel rooms in the way that the losing Argentines had. We would have come out onto the streets and confrontations would then have been inevitable. Some suggested it was because English mobile phones didn't work in Japan; others that it was the way the ordinary Japanese had welcomed all the world's fans, the English being the ones who appreciated it most because they were the largest contingent.

Whatever the reason, the Japanese discovered that the English were neither gentlemen nor hooligans. The two are nearly as far apart as it is possible for two versions of masculinity to be: one rules his passions, the other lets his passions rule him; one uses violence as a last resort, the other uses it as his first; one uses his wits, the other his fists; the one is impossible to live up to and the other is impossible to live with. By destroying England's gentleman image and then failing to substitute the hooligan in its place, by giving the English in Japan the freedom to play at being themselves, this World Cup permanently changed the Japanese view of the English.

Something very similar happened to the English who went to Japan. Except for a very few people, such as John Jones, everyone left Japan with his or her own stories of kamikaze kindnesses, the like of which they had never seen; of a carnivalesque street party that they would never forget; and of an enthusiasm for the English that they had never experienced at a football event before. Nobody who went there would ever think of the Japanese in the same way again. The country's nerdy image was gone forever.

The nerd and the hooligan are actually as far apart as it is possible for two versions of masculinity to be. But for all their differences, the nerd and the hooligan have one thing in common: they lack empathy. So it was that when the English discovered that the Japanese weren't nerds, and the Japanese discovered that the English weren't hooligans, they found an empathy that neither had expected.

At Frankfurt airport, on the way home, I met an entertainer, a Londoner who had been a redcoat, 'all Gatling mouth' as he described himself, his hand winding an imaginary lever by his cheek. He described how he had made a fat American girl in a Japanese bar cry. She deserved it, he said, for slagging off her boyfriend and being so obnoxious. Despite this he claimed 'a lot of success with the women'. He had kept away from the city centres and had stayed in the smaller towns. And he had his story of kamikaze kindness, of going into a hotel and finding it full up, of walking away only to be picked up by the hotel manager in his car and driven round the rest of the hotels in the town. He had other stories of how he had spent three days with a girl and then tired of her. They had boarded a train together and while they were waiting for it to leave he had nipped off with the excuse of getting something, and then the train had pulled out and he had waved from the platform as she left him. 'Her face . . .' but he did not describe it; he did not need to.

But then he said:

'I used to laugh at them, the Japanese tourists in London with their cameras and their maps, always getting lost, but you know what I'm going to do now? I'm going to go up to them and help them as a way of thanking them for all the help they've given me.'

And that is how Japan got him.

KICKING